To Build My Shadow a Fire

Books by David Wevill

Penguin Modern Poets 4
(with David Holbrook and Christopher Middleton) (1963)

Birth of a Shark (1964)

A Christ of the Ice-Floes (1966)

Penguin Modern European Poets: Sándor Weöres and Ferenc Juhász (1970)

Firebreak (1971)

Where the Arrow Falls (1974)

Casual Ties (1983)

Other Names for the Heart: New and Selected Poems 1964–1984 (1985)

Figure of Eight: New Poems and Selected Translations (1987)

Figure of Eight (1988)

Child Eating Snow (1994)

Solo With Grazing Deer (2001)

Departures: Selected Poems (2003)

Asterisks (2007)

TO BUILD MY SHADOW A FIRE

The Poetry and Translations
of David Wevill

Edited by Michael McGriff

Truman State University Press
New Odyssey Series

Published by Truman State University Press, Kirksville, Missouri USA
tsup.truman.edu
© 2010 Truman State University Press
New Odyssey Series
All rights reserved

Cover image: "Bizarre Tree in Front of Sand Dune," Mlenny Photography, with permission of iStockphoto.

Cover design: Teresa Wheeler
Type: Arno Pro © Adobe Systems Inc.; Galahad © Adobe Systems Inc.
Printed by: Edwards Brothers Inc., Ann Arbor, Michigan USA

Library of Congress Cataloging-in-Publication Data

Wevill, David, 1935–
To build my shadow a fire : the poetry and translations of David Wevill / David Wevill; selected, edited, and with an introduction by Michael McGriff.
        p. cm. — (New Odyssey series)
Includes index.
ISBN 978-1-935503-04-0 (pbk. : alk. paper)
1. Canadian poetry—20th century. I. McGriff, Michael, 1976– II. Title.
PR9199.3.W4257T6 2010
811'.54—dc22

                                                                        2010004300

For Mike and Britta, who lit the fire and kept it going.

I'm carried in my shadow
like a violin
in its black case.
　　　　　　　—Tomas Tranströmer

Contents

Part One 🔥 Poetry

Part Two ♭ Translations

Author's Preface

It is difficult to preface a book that covers so much of one's lifetime. The poems and other work in this selection represent some forty-five years, during which there have been many life-changes, changes of circumstance and place, especially my move from England to America in the late sixties.

There have been changes, too, in voice, style, and technique. An earlier rhetorical energy gave way to a more stripped-down, quieter economy of expression, relying more on image than descriptive elaboration. But while much has changed, weathered perhaps, some themes and preoccupations remain, I think, as ground-notes throughout. They are part of one's shadow, for better or worse, they move as one's self moves.

The poems here, I hope, speak for themselves. The short prose-form pieces are another way of speaking. The translations are occasional, except for the Juhász poems, which were commissioned by Penguin. With virtually all the translations I've needed the help of native speakers.

Lastly, and importantly, I owe this book to Michael McGriff, a fine poet and friend. He conceived it, he shaped it and put it together, and his energy, effort, and patience nursed it to publication. I owe him a very great debt of thanks.

David Wevill
Austin, Texas
September 2009

Editor's Preface

Toni Morrison has written somewhere that she began her life as a novelist when she made the simple decision to write the books that she wanted to read. I admire this sentiment as both a reader and writer—it's a warning against listening to the various taste-makers and dictators of culture, and it's a call to action, an invitation to make it new, a celebration of the individual voice. To this end, the roots of *To Build My Shadow a Fire* are straightforward. I wanted to read (and wanted to share with others) a book that didn't exist, so I had to make it myself. When I received David Wevill's blessing for this endeavor, I proceeded not as a scholar or critic (that is to say, with no formulated aesthetic agenda or tinted biographical lens), but as an avid reader and admirer of the poetry itself. I let my intuition about the work guide me during the editorial process, with David serving as both sounding board and veto holder. That said, assembling a collection like this is not simply the process of compiling the "best" work. A book of poetry (be it an edited collection or an individual volume), essentially, is a unified, sequential work, with each poem being a distinct source of light shining within a pool of light. The editorial challenge is to find the many arcs of the work, and to highlight those arcs with the most invisible of hands, for to cast a shadow or hold up a mirror does a great and potentially dangerous disservice to the writer, the reader, and ultimately, to the art itself. This invisibility act proved complicated when excerpting from the long sequences in *Firebreak, Where the Arrow Falls,* and *Asterisks*. I wanted to honor the narrative, thematic, and stylistic threads in each of these works by piecing together key sequential portions that spoke to the overall trajectory of the given piece. Though it is undeniable that the ideal and most contextualized way to enter a poet's work is to enter it in its entirety and on its own terms, and though it is the nature of a book such as this to be suggestive rather than comprehensive, it is also true that a thoughtful selection of a writer's work will open as many doors as the reader is willing to step through.

Projects like these are never tackled alone, and I have many to thank. Of course, my thanks to David Wevill for entrusting me with such a rare, important, and meaningful undertaking. Thanks to Britta Ameel, Eavan Boland, Carl Adamshick, Michael Dickman, Matthew Dickman, Charles Seluzicki, and Bruce Meyer for offering invaluable support and editorial advice. Thanks to Tony Frazer at Shearsman Books for sending me a copy of

Wevill's obscure chapbook *Figure of Eight*. I would also like to express my appreciation for Barry Callaghan and Michael Callaghan at Exile Editions Ltd.—both are long-standing champions of Wevill's poetry and deserve to be recognized for their efforts. Many heartfelt thanks to Nancy Rediger, Barbara Smith-Mandell, and Jim Barnes at Truman State University Press. Without their vision, this book would not exist.

Michael McGriff
San Francisco
September 2009

Acknowledgments

Works in this volume have been previously published in the following books:

Penguin Modern Poets 4 (Penguin, 1963)

Birth of a Shark (Macmillan, 1964)

A Christ of the Ice-Floes (Macmillan, 1966)

Penguin Modern European Poets: Sándor Weöres and Ferenc Juhász (Penguin, 1970)

Firebreak (Macmillan, 1971)

Where the Arrow Falls (Macmillan, 1974)

Casual Ties (Curbstone Publishing Company, 1983)

Other Names for the Heart: New and Selected Poems 1964–1984 (Exile Editions, 1985)

Figure of Eight: New Poems and Selected Translations (Exile Editions, 1987)

Child Eating Snow (Exile Editions, 1994)

Solo With Grazing Deer (Exile Editions, 2001)

Asterisks (Exile Editions, 2007)

Introduction

Michael McGriff

David Wevill was born a Canadian in Yokohama, Japan, where his family had lived for two generations, in 1935. His family left for Canada before the outbreak of World War II. Wevill grew up in Canada, and moved to England to attend Caius College, Cambridge, where he graduated with honors in English and history (M.A.) in 1958. During the 1960s Wevill lived in London, Burma (where he taught at the University of Mandalay for two years), and Spain. He moved to Texas in 1968, where he joined the Department of English at the University of Texas at Austin. He became a dual citizen (Canada and the United States) in 1994, and taught in the English department at Texas until his retirement in 2007. He continues to reside in Austin.

Wevill gained recognition as a promising new voice during his involvement with the rich poetry culture surrounding the University of Cambridge in the late 1950s. Four of Wevill's earliest published poems are found in *Poetry from Cambridge: 1958* (Fortune Press, 1958). In addition to Wevill, twenty-one poets comprise *Poetry from Cambridge,* most notably Sylvia Plath, Robert Wallace, and Ted Hughes. More notoriously, Wevill was associated with The Group, an unofficial "workshop" collective of young poets in London. Whether by design or by chance, the poems generated by The Group served as a stark contrast to the creative efforts generated by the so-called Movement. The Movement poets were featured in Robert Conquest's 1956 *New Lines* anthology (Macmillan) and tended toward a conservative, somewhat neoclassical, and traditionally formal aesthetic. The Group was facilitated by Philip Hobsbaum in 1954, then by Edward Lucie-Smith in 1959. The ranks of The Group included an ever-shifting amalgamation of young poets whose origins were as varied as Pakistan, Australia, Cyprus, and Jamaica. In addition to Wevill, The Group facilitated, to varying degrees, the creative efforts of Zulfikar Ghose, George MacBeth, Peter Porter, Peter Redgrove, Fleur Adcock, and Nathaniel Tarn. When Hobsbaum left Cambridge to lecture at Queen's College, Belfast, he organized the so-called Belfast Group. During its tenure, The Belfast Group included, among others, Seamus Heaney, Michael Longley, Ciarán Carson, and Paul Muldoon. In 1963 Edward Lucie-Smith and Philip Hobsbaum edited *A Group Anthology* (Oxford University Press), which included five poems by David Wevill, the anthology's lone North American voice.

England's early 1960s gave rise to one of the most influential English-language poetry venues in the postwar era, the Penguin Modern Poets series. Eschewing the traditional hardbound single-author volume, Penguin published three authors in each of its Modern Poets titles, all of which were sold as inexpensive pocket-sized paperbacks. From 1962 to 1979, Penguin published eighty-one poets (twenty-seven books) in this format, including Lawrence Durrell, Allen Ginsberg, William Carlos Williams, Charles Bukowski, John Ashbery, Edwin Muir, Kenneth Koch, and Denise Levertov, as well as several poets featured in *A Group Anthology*. The fourth title in this series, *Penguin Modern Poets 4* (Penguin, 1963), showcased the poetry of David Holbrook, Christopher Middleton, and David Wevill. In this volume, readers first caught a broader glimpse of Wevill's distinct style, which is marked by a controlled, muscular line, dark and earthy imagery, and a lyrical voice that speaks from the empirical world as it leaps toward the realm of the figurative. We can see these traits in the opening and final stanzas of Wevill's first poem in *Penguin Modern Poets 4*, "The Two-Colored Eagle."

> The last days wrenched her inward completely.
> Her beak scraped inner brain,
> Her skull turned to old rocks and the wine seeped out dry.
>
> . . . .
>
> Now her iron-age furnace heart
> Hardens too, with October, the dead in our bones.
> It is a grim place to bring love.

The speaker in these poems, and to a larger extent in the later work, finds himself out in the wilderness, sorting through his desires and fears amid an organic, uncontrollable, and oftentimes violent terrain. In this metaphorical territory, the voice wears the mask of the pilgrim, the exile, and the Orphic figure.

One year after the publication of *Penguin Modern Poets 4*, Wevill produced his first full-length collection, *Birth of a Shark* (Macmillan, 1964). This book contains the best work in *Penguin Modern Poets 4* and an ample selection of new work. *Birth of a Shark* resonates both tonally and thematically with his first publication, continuing the search to create a language for the precarious relationship between death, life, and the elemental. As seen in the following excerpts from the long poem "Fugue for Wind and Rain," the voice has the capacity to become a synthesis of man and landscape, both of which are acted upon by a sense of darkness, isolation, and danger.

> We come into a new time; the heavy-mooned
> Darkness hangs its orange crater flare
> Above the sea.
> My beaches are quiet: not a crab
> Shuffles to disgorge its load of soft bulk from its outworn
> Shell and die
> In patterns on the sand. ...
> . . . .

> We come into a new time,
> The world and myself: ...

> . . . .

> ... In my effort to call them back
> I make slaves of everything I see: that ditch
> Where wineskin-fat cactuses gripped
> The white solid fortress rock,
> Where red-black beetles fought and tore at each other's
> Strung nerves: in the violence of thunder off the hills'
> One rainstorm in a month,—
> In our bodies gored by the flame of July night.

> . . . .

> This sea has many coasts,
> And every inch and brown pool
> Is a fingerprint.

> . . . .

... I look for the change of light, now
Over this sea: which tomorrow promises only by small chance
To reveal, be re-revealed
Through its weak heart of water, my body, my blood.

Birth of a Shark was greeted with critical acclaim in the UK, and quickly went into a second printing. In 1965, *Birth of a Shark* garnered the Arts Council Book Prize for the best first or second book published in the three previous years (an award shared with Philip Larkin for his collection *The Whitsun Weddings*), the Richard Hillary Prize, and an Arts Council Poetry Bursary.

For Wevill, 1966 marked a meteoric year. His work was showcased in the revised and enlarged edition of A. Alvarez's seminal anthology, *The New Poetry* (Oxford University Press, 1966); he published his second full-length collection, *A Christ of the Ice-Floes* (Macmillan, 1966); he was awarded a second Arts Council Poetry Bursary; and *A Christ of the Ice-Floes* was runner-up for Canada's Governor General's Award (which Margaret Atwood won for *The Circle Game*). In addition to the poetry showcased in *The New Poetry*, Alvarez's truculent, finger-pointing introduction to the anthology, "Beyond the Gentility Principle," helped to make the book both an instant controversy and an instant success (*The New Poetry* eventually sold over 150,000 copies). In "Beyond the Gentility Principle," he railed against the decency, politeness, and bourgeois conservatism he found at play in the English poets of the postwar era, particularly the Movement poets:

> Of the nine poets to appear in this [*New Lines*], six, at the time,
> were university teachers, two librarians, and one a Civil Servant.
> It was, in short, academic-administrative verse, polite, knowledge-
> able, efficient, polished, and, in its quiet way, even intelligent.
> What it had to offer positively was more difficult to describe.

In its first edition, *The New Poetry* postured itself as an all-English anthology, though it contained the work of American poets Robert Lowell and John Berryman. In short, *The New Poetry* featured the poets who would define their generation: Donald Davie, Philip Larkin, Michael Hamburger, Christopher Middleton, Charles Tomlinson, Thom Gunn, Ted Hughes, Geoffrey Hill, George MacBeth, Ian Hamilton. In its revised and enlarged edition, *The New Poetry* shed its English-only parameters, adding Sylvia Plath, Anne

Sexton, Peter Porter, and David Wevill to its table of contents.

A Christ of the Ice-Floes follows the trajectory of Wevill's previous work, yet it differs in three ways. The poems in this volume, arguably, are his most distinctly Canadian—not in the sense of nationalism or populism, but in the sense that many of the poems deal directly with details of landscape and place exclusive to the Canada of the author's adolescence. Secondly, the poems in this collection signal the beginning of Wevill's experiment with the fragment and poetic line, as seen here in "Either/Or."

> I
>
>   you
>
>   witnesses—
>
> the doors between us   glass doors
> through the clothes and skin
>   and the senses'
>   circuit
> from event to event
>   are interlocking circles
>   never concentric
> never the same wound in the same place
>   but a shift in the air
> like a mouth riding alone   through the spaces
>   of rooms: speaking
> whisper-cautions   less than that   lip-readings
>
> . . . .
>
> I fret for the future   but am at peace in the now
>   and no new thing
>   can blend us or divide us
>   beyond what we are
> and will be.

Thirdly, this volume marks Wevill's first explicit engagement with the ethical dilemmas surrounding modernization, mechanization, and the environment, themes that appear, in varying degrees, throughout the rest of his published works. These concerns are explicit in "Wherever Men Have Been," the penultimate poem in this collection.

In 1968 Wevill made the enormous move from London to Austin, where he joined the University of Texas at Austin's Department of English. It is difficult to imagine what it must have been like for a Canadian national whose previous residences included Japan, Burma, Spain, and England to move to the United States during the height of both the unpopular war in Vietnam and the cultural radicalism of the 1960s, let alone to the utterly alien landscape of the American Southwest. In 1970 Wevill published a translation of Hungarian poet Ferenc Juhász's selected poems in the Penguin Modern European Poets series, one of the most important and influential translation venues for the English-speaking poetry community in the second half of the twentieth century. The poets in the Penguin Modern European Poets series, several of whom made an appearance in an English trade edition for the first time, have become the essential poetic voices of our modern era. Volumes in this series included work by Zbigniew Herbert, Vasko Popa, Anna Akhmatova, Dan Pagis, Giuseppe Ungaretti, Alexander Blok, Tomas Tranströmer, Guillaume Apollinaire, Marina Tsvetayeva, Fernando Pessoa, Yehuda Amichai, Paul Celan, Miroslav Holub, Yevgeny Yevtushenko, Cesare Pavese, Yannis Ritsos, and several Nobel Laureates, including Nelly Sachs, Günter Grass, Eugenio Montale, Joseph Brodsky, Odysseus Elytis, Salvatore Quasimodo, and George Seferis. Wevill's Juhász translations are included in one the most comprehensive anthologies of Hungarian poetry and poetics, *In Quest of the Miracle Stag: The Poetry of Hungary; An Anthology of Hungarian Poetry from the 13th Century to the Present in English Translation Vol. 1*, edited by Adam Makkai (Tertia, 1996).

A firebreak (also called a fire line, fire road, or fuel brake) is a section of ground cleared of vegetation that acts as a natural barrier to an approaching wildfire. With the publication of *Firebreak* (Macmillan, 1971), it's as if the poet scraped a line into the earth, stepped across it, and said, "I am going deeper into myself." With the American Southwest as its backdrop, *Firebreak* is a volume haunted by apparitions and psychic pain. This elliptical, book-length sequence is wrought with elegiac tones, circuitous patterns, cryptic narrative elements, and images of place that converge to create a lyrical underworld where the speaker confronts his separation from the "other." This other takes the form of the feminine, yet it also reflects a sense of tragic otherness within the speaker himself. This book stands out among Wevill's work in that it represents a figure in a moment of true crisis, a voice searching for life within fragments and ruins. This collection lies hinged upon a tipping point, and as the book unfolds the speaker journeys toward the renewal that the image of a firebreak embodies.

Where the Arrow Falls (Macmillan, 1974) is a book-length sequence comprising three long sections, the first two of which are poetry, and the third lyric prose. This wide-ranging collection is held together under the vast net of its title, which Wevill explains in the following excerpt from an interview he gave for Bruce Meyer's *Lives and Works* (Black Moss Press, 1992).

> The title comes from a Persian story of the king who had three sons. He told his sons to shoot their arrows into the air and to build their palaces where the arrows fell. This worked all right for two of them. They built their palaces, married, and lived happily ever after. But the third one, his arrow disappeared, and to find it he had to go on a magical journey, which involved ordeals. But when he accomplished it he had so much more than the rest of them.

Though similar in tone to *Firebreak*, this collection rests on a concept that gives Wevill a vessel capable of including anything, and this inclusive impulse makes for an unpredictable and expansive volume. Wevill manages to draw upon sources as different as Francisco Goya, various symbolic animals, János Pilinzski, the Mayans, multiple tricksters, Persian and Greek mythology, Igor Stravinsky, and American Indians such as the Cheyenne, Tlingit, Yaqui, Hopi, and Navajo. Throughout this sequence, Wevill often grounds the reader in one setting then jumps to another, giving *Where the Arrow Falls* a kinetic and unpredictable feel. One of the many examples of this is section 16 of *Part One,* where the poem unfolds as a meditation on a rotting water moccasin then leaps into a meditation where the speaker addresses the Hungarian poet János Pilinzski:

Cottonmouth
dead
with a hole
in your side

flies at the closed mouth
flies at the hole

even now
I wouldn't touch you

olive, with rusty bands
the slit eye
only a picture of watching

broken *S*
shape in the stony dust
far from water, where your bite is worst
in death, venomous still
as ripped from the living

—Pilinzski, patient Hungarian
I have your papers on my desk

to try and bring you alive
this day the snake died
in this dust, Harbach
cripple

venom
in memories … stones
of dry Texas, not

those dark potato fields
where prisoners crept

between wires hung with scorpions
and daybreak, the spirit's release

into no new world

The experiment of this volume, in part, is to find meaning at the confluence of one's obsessions and one's surroundings, and to bear witness to the mysteries of such a union.

In 1983, Austin-based Curbstone Publishing Company[1] released Wevill's *Casual Ties,* a book-length sequence of thirty-three linked prose poems. Like much of his work, *Casual Ties* is image-driven and uroboric, yet this collection unearths new ground. Wevill's experiment within the tradition of the prose poem allows him to follow his philosophical lines of inquiry with a newfound sense of invention and intellectual play. This play takes the form of riddles, parables, confrontations with unlikely tricksters (a pushy scrap of paper), and it ultimately gives Wevill a platform to question the limits of language, space and time, and existence itself. Despite its explicitly intellectual nature, Wevill avoids striking academic or lofty tones in *Casual Ties.* In fact, the writing is largely conversational, witty, and surreal, with a sense of the magical and meta-fictional tempering the work.

The new work in both *Other Names for the Heart: New and Selected Poems 1964–1984* (Exile Editions, 1985) and *Figure of Eight: New Poems and Selected Translations* (Exile Editions, 1987) represents an aesthetic shift in Wevill's poetry. Several of Wevill's themes and images resurface in this work, yet they occur in poems making the move from a more fragmentary and lyrically explosive style to one containing a more traditionally delivered syntax, with lines tending toward the left margin, and with the image more controlled. "Shallots" is an example of this shift.

She dreamt
her tongue was made of mud.
When she spoke
the little shell-like syllables fell apart
as her tongue dissolved, no one

understood her. In the rain
her eyes stood as two pools

---

[1]Curbstone Publishing Company should not be confused with Curbstone Press, the noted publisher of Latin American and Latino literature based in Willimantic, Connecticut. Curbstone Publishing Company was a short-lived press (eleven books by nine authors from 1978 to 1986) whose experimental fiction and poetry titles are long out of print and increasingly uncommon. Curbstone Publishing Company's roster included, among others, Stuart Peterfreund, Willis Barnstone, Geraldine Little, and Zulfikar Ghose.

where someone's fingers had poked holes
and left them for the tide to fill.

Now
her children wonder where their mother went.
They finger their eyelids tentatively and
curl their tongues in the soft earth of speech

and breathe quickly, like children treading water.

The work in these two titles retains the inclusive and allusive impulses the poet sharpens in *Where the Arrow Falls,* yet the work has a drastically different feel. One of Wevill's gifts, indeed, is the re-examination of obsessions—and in this volume, we see familiar emotional and philosophical landscapes, yet we see them anew through the stylistic tilt given to the work.

Child Eating Snow (Exile Editions, 1994) and *Solo With Grazing Deer* (Exile Editions, 2001) feel as if they are two volumes comprising the same vast and searching book. The poems in both collections range from the mundane and outward to the private and inward. One defining feature of these two collections is Wevill's explicit political engagement with the global tragedies of the twentieth century. Throughout his career, Wevill enters his poetry with a certain sense of darkness, but his sense of tragedy often spells itself out in terms of the psychic and internal. In *Child Eating Snow,* poems such as "Bettelheim" and "Ethnic Poem II" bear witness to the unnecessary suffering of children. In "Exuberance (Paul Klee)," the voice in the poem foretells an era of brownshirts and genocide.

… it was 1939
I failed to see the hidden
woman shawled in dark blue mourning
in one corner
I failed to see
dead center
the booted man in brown with huge shoulders
beginning to scream at me

Wevill's poems of witness never use a heavy hand, nor do they tend toward the didactic. More importantly, they refuse to allow the speaker to stand outside of history. In "Exuberance (Paul Klee)," it is what the speaker *fails* to see that foretells what our century will see. We are flawed, Wevill suggests, and we have the inherent capacity to fail each other on both a personal and global scale. In *Solo With Grazing Deer,* the theme of colossal human failure appears in the poem "Lamp."

> While I was dreaming inside my flame
> the wind bit at the edges of my teeth
> and I thought I could see in the dark—
> it was your word against mine.
>
> Though they had broken shattered pieced together
> Dresden and Hiroshima
> Coventry London Guernica
> the shadows you left wouldn't move.
>
> So in Robert Capa's photograph
> of a street in Bilbao in 1936
> eight women and men and a young girl
> look up at the sky at where German bombers
>
> are coming. So it might have been
> a little before dawn when a boy not quite one
> woke up in a white crib in Yokohama
> and saw shadows cross the ceiling of his room
>
> —the world had soft bones
> and old and brittle bones
> and from time to time the light falls
> exactly where the body runs to hide.

In his 1987 *Lives and Works* interview, Wevill discusses the impact of growing up bilingual in Japan, as well as the general impact of Asian poetry on his work. He surmises that one cultural and artistic element inherent to Asian poetry is its capacity to produce and embody "the presence of space and silence. The presence of absence." "The real effort," Wevill asserts, "is to make present something which is both silent and soft-spoken, and the laconic genius in that." These words, spoken over twenty years ago, best describe the work from his most recent collection, *Asterisks* (Exile Editions, 2007), a pared-down, lyrical sequence of forty-nine numbered poems. As a typographical symbol, an asterisk (from the Latin *asteriscum*, meaning "little star") can indicate a footnote, a jump in thought or scene, an omission, a change in subject, a particular trait or special circumstance, a leap. This collection, then, is a series of leaping encounters between the poet and his center, with each poem, or asterisk, serving as a different referential and lyrical mirror for the speaker. Some asterisks refer to the known, such as the speaker's "singular addiction / to old wounds" (section 19), whereas others grapple with the uncertain, such as the quest to define one's poetics. Wevill's combination of form and obsession also plays out in this collection. As seen in section 9, the poet seeks to create a space that will contain his images and ideas, the most dominant of which is the feminine ghost that haunts and sustains so much of his poetic landscape.

> This mark refers you to
> another place
>   fire, her star
> an unpronounceable name
> whose wherebeing
>   kept old light
>
> She had a way with her
> What lovers saw
>   or missed
> in her eyes
> was an ancient event
> a murdered light
>   gone black
>
> Texture of an empty chair
>
> vacated air.

The work featured in *To Build My Shadow a Fire* moves like the minimalist compositions of Arvo Pärt—there are dark, essential notes, and they are summoned time and again with a deliberate hand. There are resurfacings and tessellations. With each repetition a new dimension of the work is revealed, a new facet of an obsession held up to the light, and the closer the artist journeys through the layers of the self toward the mysteries of his impulses, the shadow at the center of his being.

Part One   Poetry

From *Penguin Modern Poets 4* (1963)

The Two-Colored Eagle

The last days wrenched her inward completely.
Her beak scraped inner brain,
Her skull turned to old rocks and the wine seeped out dry.

Under her hooded scrutiny now
The Rhine flows on, without help; she can't stop it.
In the perfect dead breathless quiet
Her only sound is the blind deep drumming of barges
Tugging her weight, tapping
Northwards, against the current.

Snow must fall like bone-meal here,
And success fledges no new eagles. We paw
In the cold, towards her warm red side
Of sunset, where the aching black
Grapes shiver their tinsel warnings at birds.
On either side her wings are folded, hard.
Her back is against the south,
Her brackish beak is raised to the North Sea.

Now her iron-age furnace heart
Hardens too, with October, the dead in our bones.
It is a grim place to bring love.

My Father Sleeps

Who brought from the snow-wrecked
Hulk of winter his salvaged
Purpose; who came, blind but friendly
By these lines his mouth and his eyes

Have fixed; and without further talk
Taught me at last how to walk,
Until by his power I came
Out of innocence like the worm's flame
Into daylight. What practical need
His patience had, and anger bred
Of disillusionment, has gone with age.
I have this white-haired image,
Arrogant perhaps, and too much the hero
For our friendship's good: Lear, although
Afraid of words as of madness,
Of procrastination as of disease—
A lover of plain-spokenness—
Though not where it hurt, that he could understand.
If I trace the scars in my right hand
They tell me of purpose disobeyed,
Of old and factual truths my head
Cannot alter. And watching him thus
Sprawled like a crooked frame of clothes
In the sleep of sixty years, jaws firm,
Breathing through the obstacle of his nose
A stubborn air that is truth for him,
I confront my plainest self. And feel
In the slow hardening of my bones, a questioning
Depth that his pride could never reveal;
That in his sleep stirs its cruel beginning.

Spiders

Muddling up the wooden stairs one night, in my socks
Past screens and shuttered bunting-creviced wallboards,
My tongue dry, but a cool wind puffing thinly soft

Up my torn shirt-front, the dust hot-thick in my hair,
I crossed my sister coming that way in her slip—
The steep way down, half-asleep; her chicken-hearted breathing
And toes antennaed for spiders or bits of fluff
That might jiggle and spill a mouse. I tasted my own breath
Kekking, milkweed-sour, after the beer—
But not to budge, or her shriek might wake the house—
Who is it! I didn't know her face—
Such full pails for eyes; she might have been glass;
The roman nose, pink lips peeled white over salt
While ten years woke up and started ... I thought myself
Back, a loiterer in jeans, hands spittled with oil
From throbbing handlebars. Wind shoulders the porch,
Flickers the close trees.... I held back then
And jammed my buttocks hard against black wood,
My back a prickly heat of rusty nails which
Builders'd slapped in, and left, when the lake was young
With all her forests open to the wind, mated conifers
Exploding dry cones. I listened in the dark,
And thought, this wife won't wait to be woken by me,
But go on down, passing me, always on my left—
Wind clacking the picture-frames through our big house—
I wasn't going to wake her. I mightn't have seemed
Her brother, then, but eight legs sprung on her dream,
Something she'd sense far worse than spiders, on the stair,
That could harm her children. Maybe it wasn't just fear,
Or concern, that made me cringe from her.
Two people who cross in the dark walk nearest to ghosts,
Her terror might have stuck its mouth in me,
And sealed her against a love she could not cope with,
Grinning under heavy sheets, with her heartbeat.

Last Settlers

Whoever lived in this house commanded the valley,
Hawk-wheel and crow-glide, all his. Ten miles
From heel to lip and steep-ravined,
Farming made hard by nettle-spike and rains;
Slope-shouldered, bow-legged men, mules, lanterns—

He planted tea. But nowhere in the scrub
Boulder or rock-fall water, now, do his whims
Outlast the jungle. Machines
Litter and rust the dry yard; her womanly cannas
Nick the blown grey valley to uncertain crimson—

Huddle like bathers. Behind its locked
Windows the house will age; worms
Freckle the weatherboard with statements, words
Phrasing their dumb tenancy, stunned
Like these veering kites that soar and press
To a tremble at the roofed hill's lip—

No settling there safe enough yet to evade
The militant dog-print on the lawn, or rash
Quipping of parrots, emerald-backed
And canna-crested; who mock that couple-voiced
Going from these heights, these pounding shores of wind.

Monsoon

for Zulfikar Ghose

A snake emptied itself into the grass.
A lizard wriggled out of a cup of ferns.

The pebbles, quiet, but nudging to follow the dust
Downwind, struggled with consciences,
Vaulting back as the gust, passing, kinked the long grass.
Then first we heard it, the long rush and rake
Abrading, stripping the earth's back, as the rain
Trailing its millions of wires, and voiding first
The lecture hall, the library and bungalows—
All the gardens springing taut, and the tennis courts
Smudged like wrecks at sea—the downpour came,
Caving its seething wall onto our verandahs,
Submerging the whole house. And we froze,
Like water-spiders clenched in their sacs of breathing,
Crouched, dry and firm in the damp close mouth of the wind,
As the tropics snapped and tore at our moderate blood—

Then after an hour the ground steamed openly.
The rain, flickering northwards into the shallow hills
Left little puddles behind, rubies aflame
In the fattened grasses drinking the sunset down,
Deep, through stem and root, and into the cave of stone
Where the scorpion hungers, carrying his bruise down.

The Venturers

I pull the blankets close, so she'll keep warm;
Their soft bulk sliding off like unroofed snow
Woke me from my dream: a quarrel of pigeons
Collapsing off the eaves, clattered into the night
And to what high homing under the eagle stars
And avalanche, flapped across the Milky Way;
Their wings luff with the curtains, my bloodbeat.

From *Penguin Modern Poets 4* (1963)

Their going's not worth regret I think, lying here;
To nest on the hilltops, muscling up supplies,
The air's skate and stumble, up the most difficult track
To the hearth and mouth. But tempers break
With the animal back; the bull's pizzle and the thorns
Can goad me only higher, beyond all goals;
And the hobble and jess of her hand on me
Cannot be let go, or lost. The dark chimes four

From a neighbor's clock. Crunch of the first tires
On the ice-rutted snow, the waking birds, will begin;
And others, rending beyond their lit eyelids will
Bury the beaks behind, the squirrel's shrill claws
That twitch my hand against her sleeping side.
And fires will knot the clockhands to hard worms,
Our earth's focus still: my crouched two eyes
Staring into the dark that is dark within;
And hers locked shut on a sleep where daylight spins
Words in the dream-kept head, bright stolen world.

Separation

Jetties suck, suck.
The broken and muddy water grips
Without purpose. The water has
Nowhere else to go, like ships.

Derricks could be of flesh
But seen through, X-rayed to the bone.
A gaunt skyline geometry,
Abstracts jerking out of human

Eyes a like jaggedness.
I imagine I see you borne
Bobbing on the brown water,
Your round eyes grey under the cold horn

Of the fog. And I touch
The river as if skin met skin,
A body identified
But crabbed, gelid, a frayed fraction,

A hermit grip rising out of the mud.
The parcel of sky, crammed, undelivered
Rains. All across the water
Tugs steam like burning dead.

In an instant the flayed river
Hisses up to the jetties
Crawling as if on legs. The ridge
Of that far bank disappears.

The river's itself. Your head
Bending down over the lettered keys
In your factory-loud office, feels
The waters surge back. You close your eyes.

Impression During an Interview

Both will lose face. The one
Nursing an idiocy
Unwinding his every word as if
The man he questioned was himself;

Gently, the gambit now a smile,
Wax to betray the mind's keyhole.

The other beginning to grope
For some brief abrading curse, which,
Circling, echoes back and back,
Through the multiple cancer that
Soars and lugs its steel-concrete
Dimension over both,
Like a broken and heavy wing,
Or a man's skull licked bare.

Clean Break

All winter the thudding sparrows came and went,
Despoiling our bread-crumb sill. And I lay in a sweat,
Watching them peck out, bit by bit,
The fabulous plenty of my heart.

Imagining their worst plight, I thought, my mind must break,
Imagining their budded claws, like scaffolding
Scrapping above the snow, and the bodies under the snow,
I lay, and could not dream;

And could not think. My brain refused such food,
But only lay and stared, until the walls, returning
Like an eavesdropping squad of surgeons, hemmed me in;
And I groped for signs of age, a first white hair…

Knowing, a man pays dearly who seldom thinks,
By having his thinking done for him;

Which is about as pleasant a trait as
Being cuckolded.

Now, in the warmth around me the rosebuds break alight;
My flesh glows dense; my arms, hooked like sickles
Encircle and clutch them; bindweed, lupins, roots
Bitter as scammony, and the touch-me-not
Barbed squiggles of the centipedes' horned fingers.

All day the earth's on fire; I burn
With the damp rheumatisms of the loam,
A dense hydrangea-head among the tougher skulls,
Feeling the leather-jackets nip under the grass,

Under the winds that jump the furrows and tracks,
Winnowing slowly like a thresher at half-speed;

And lie, and gaze up at the sun where butter melts
Drop by drop on my hands, and stings, but heals.

Puddles

I cannot comfortably gaze at standing water.
Some focus seems to lie drowned there and waiting,
Eyeing upwards, among empty shells and bottle-caps,
At the waste features of the poring sky.
If clouds unbent at this moment and dazzled it grey
This deep puddle'd split, diminish, and with a gulp
Involve me, so my lancing fury'd break its bottom
Clean as a cupcrack—What would drain

Out, the weight of water, slimy tension of skin,
Might rise to collect me, much later,
And suddenly, when I'm feverish or weak.

At Rideau Falls

The tideless Ottawa is small
Beside the rivers of old Capitals;
Is logged by nylon-shirted men,
Match-makers. At Rideau Falls
I watch, drunk, the thrust of a barge
Bruising my ribs with each lurch, coils
Of surf stampeding up the night.
I will not come back. My time
Outlingers cities; my warm children
Rest surely in my head. They will own
This germ of me that failed to grow.
They will pick stark fables from my bones.

The Crèche

The crèche of faces, like wintering crocuses, lay mute under their cauls of
white wool. I stood at the extreme end of the room, facing the wide fis-
sured mirror, and tried to identify one child that had its fingers twisted to a
hard ball in the rough smock of homespun the nuns had sewn him into.

This one, I knew, was not pitted and scarred like the others, but would have slept in a silksoft crib and blue initialed sheets in the now heavily shelled château. The lamps, looking like nuns' wimples, hung over the stark lines of cots, stiff and crisp, starched cotton such as I'd dreamed of, feeling the lice nip deep in my thick socks, touching tenderly the crescent weal on my belly where the rat had clung scrabbling with its claws.

His face, I sensed, would be free of scars and sores, something perhaps crying a little, softly, to itself, that its guardians could not get at now to retrieve. In the glaring silence of the fusty ward I could still, though barely, hear the seventy-fives, and the bigger guns, one-five-fives and naval guns, and the heavy soft flocculent heave of the mortar-bursts. Looking more intently now, I realized there wasn't time, that soon the tanks, the armored cars, and the Taubes would be circling the village, and an inky smoke would blot up all daylight at the wire-barred windows of the room, making further searches impractical.

So I shouted out my own name; and the long cot lines froze suddenly still, as if the first mortar shell had just now snapped the roof. But nothing moved or spoke, or cried even, and I saw that the nuns had gone away taking their clay jars and crucifixes with them, out of the village. The face I was searching for lay there, among the others, undiscoverable; and sleeping, I imagined, but with its pink shocked mouth open wide on a high silent wailing that followed me, like the sharp tuning-forks of bullets striking the wires, as I stumbled out into the soft April mud, haunted and nameless, as before, belonging nowhere.

From *Birth of a Shark* (1964)

Poem

I am alone in body:
My love is an outrider
Who scorns my cores of frost,
Wanders south along old lines
With her soul wrapped in furs....
Change is change,
It cannot be forced or adored
For better, for worse.

You walk in loudening circles around me,
Licking the treetop-shattered wind
For empty sustenance.
Your trail is subtle,
And in this cold
No scent carries.

Germinal

Wastes grow; you lean into the sun
As towards a good husband, hoping its fire
Will incinerate your trash and not you.

Above us the dogged stars sweat and freeze,
Mimicking suns. Who can they be,
These germless, clean immortals?
They suffer laws beyond our laws—

Strictures, paradox. Devils play
In the hair of the hillside, if you look too close.

The sun seeps into and through your bones,
Flushing the clotted soil,
Tapping bacteria, mites, and the locked
Purses of beetles. And you, fiery and whole

Are pure waste matter, aged to a diamond's strength;
Your will and body, stone and root,
Mind playing the manager, body the staff
That bears it.

   —Listen to me now;
I bring my life to you, like a petition
Expecting an answer. Heart and heart,
Beating in the one way of hearts,
Earthward, my founding engine.

Under the slipshod leaves beaten to leather
With the thawing March rain, relaxed
As only the warmth and wet can relax—
Fur, nails, sinuses, muscles—
Don't choose your first-found patch of bones
For the coffin of our vows.

I feed on your wastes, as nothing can on perfection
But must starve, or go bad
In its own time, so brimming with its death.

Let me carry your wastes through my mouth,
Carefully, as a cat lifts its young;
Or better, as a she-goat eats her afterbirth,

Assuming to herself her rightful body,
Without regret or distaste,
Certain of her ways, if not their names.

Fraying-Stocks

I am tall as this ruined tower
Or short as this grassblade. Traveling the sun's
Arc, I am neither.
Just my shadow changing height with the day.

I have witnesses. The falcon,
The May-beetle's grubs; these,
And the thumping feet of dancers have broken me open.

Walking between trees, hawthorn
And elm in an April downpour, I grow
A black glistening coat of bark—
No disguise but a kind of touch;
My rings of parsnip iron
Could be mistaken for grief around the eyes.

Soon, when the weather breaks
I'll go. Already the sap pushes a hard
Corolla of nails over my flowering jaws.
Face of hectic white—

Blood familiar to blackflies—

The treacherous nearness of life
Under surfaces trained to hold and protect,
Embarrassed by the green eyes of ponds,
Outstares the clocks of cities,—

A ritual sickness grows
In the antler's shape; breaks with my flight;
But is cured by no
Thoughts of returning, no hope of change.

A Legend

The sinewy nerves of a cabbage now
Contain my head. Its pulse-count
Falls to a trickle, under the icing of hope.

I am more things than a vegetable,
Or a landscape battered blue by March;
I run over them. I perpetrate
Cruelties at their roots. And still they follow
Their needs and ways: burns
Heal in the generations, old wounds grow stony
And bother nothing but the mind.

Through it all, my telltale streaks in the wind
From her quarter. I am more
Than these things. Who would judge my secrets?

So I wake one morning, and tell my legs
Of the difficult journey made
Aghast in the dream. How small I must make myself!
And how great—

With catastrophe! The beating of rain
Eats into the sun's thaw. I have gathered wood
To build my shadow a fire—
Is she female? At lunch I chew my meat
Slowly, wondering if I am vegetarian.

I nibble dryly at crusts and become
The whole, huskless grain before an aching fire.
A pride like mine must have
More lives in its hands than one,

And in such generous variety that
The stars seem egotistical. Who would complain

Of the number of swordblades and plowblades
Through which the earthworm now
Pushes his waste? And still

The deserted, the dead, and the blind go underground,
To weep at these monstrous remains
That never grew in them.

I watch them now;
My altars of fire and sunlight become
Too crowded with worshippers. I go down
Hoping, Eurydice, to find you there.

Wine-Cask

What is blacker than a black horse,
The coffin seems to ask;
Unless it is the shadow of this church.
Nothing is blacker than this doorway—
Even in England they can't
Manufacture such a depth of black.
Why must they carry my black oak
Through the sunlight, on their high shoulders.
Why not just let me slip
This bulk loose, and return to the forced root?
"This contrast," the mourners say,
"Is necessary for our friend's beginning.
He must make a new start—
Patterns on the sand in the sunlight.

Take the brightest and darkest of life
And bury them together.
Meanwhile we wear our mourning
Between dawn and twilight,
Shaved chins and veils over our moles."

Fugue for Wind and Rain

We come into a new time; the heavy-mooned
Darkness hangs its orange crater flare
Above the sea.
My beaches are quiet: not a crab
Shuffles to disgorge its load of soft bulk from its outworn
Shell and die
In patterns on the sand. Tonight
The wind sickens with heat: late strollers loaf
And stumble over curbs; and all
Earth's energy's coiled with this soaking sheet wrung
From the insomniac's dreamed sleep of the windstorm.

We come into a new time,
The world and myself: parable of the dog
Who buried his sense of smell with the bone-scraps,
And could find neither.
Consuls, lictors, slaves—
Dipped in Caesar's blood, blood of the fishes;
Men and their knives of rule, manners, lives, hypocrisy
Of bride and groom, ride on
Bloodily to rebirths. In my effort to call them back
I make slaves of everything I see: that ditch
Where wineskin-fat cactuses gripped
The white solid fortress rock,

Where red-black beetles fought and tore at each other's
Strung nerves: in the violence of thunder off the hills'
One rainstorm in a month,—
In our bodies gored by the flame of July night.

Night along the sea promenade,
Black as my boots and finer than hair,
Drifts with the flickering torches of ships towards that far
White mustering of daybreak—
Time of the Greeks and before, the sea, these coasts
A haze of bound chapters now.
Over this nurturing ache of black
Nothing breaks; but is made to know its final breakage plain
And whole as a part
Of the fissure it came from. I look,
And can see no change: but am myself
The sign itself of change in everything: the clean, sharp
Fissure that bleeds the cactus, the deadly
Rote and scrabble of the red
Beetles spitting out their eggs …

Storm draw the water out of me.

This sea has many coasts,
And every inch and brown pool
Is a fingerprint. The gannets come
Plunging, wreck their sight; the sea-salt keeps
The crab-flesh it corrodes; and the grape-
Avenging Dog-star locks
These fiery lives to the pillows we drown on.
Age has its lovers:
And neither history nor bad experience can ever redeem my one
Fault-finding
First error. I look for the change of light, now

Over this sea: which tomorrow promises only by small chance
To reveal, be re-revealed
Through its weak heart of water, my body, my blood.

Third Time Lucky

Twice I called, and twice
A surging upcrack wave bundled my voice
And all my belongings away out of earshot.
I stood alone in the sea,
Up to my neck in the swirl—
And called, not helplessly,
But as a man calls who has been denied
Too often to want his echo to obey;
And rages with his head
Under the feeling pulse of stars,
To that emptiness where sounds break—

Rose, and clawed my way to the sand,
And a meal of crabs, fish-heads; violence
Lying scattered and dead at my feet,
From the sea's last wave, barest returns.

The Birth of a Shark

What had become of the young shark?
It was time for the ocean to move on.
Somehow, sheathed in the warm current
He'd lost his youthful bite, and fell
Shuddering among the feelers of kelp

And dragging weeds. His belly touched sand,
The shark ran aground on his shadow.

Shark-shape, he lay there.
But in the world above
Six white legs dangled, thrashing for the fun of it,
Fifty feet above the newborn shadow.

The shark nosed up to spy them out;
He rose slowly, a long grey feather
Slendering up through the dense air of the sea.
His eyes of bolted glass were fixed
On a roundness of sun and whetted flesh,
Glittering like stars above his small brain—

The shark rose gradually. He was half-grown,
About four feet: strength of a man's thigh
Wrapped in emery, his mouth a watery
Ash of brambles. As he rose
His shadow paled and entered the sand,
Dissolved, in the twinkling shoals of driftsand
Which his thrusting tail spawned.

This was the shark's birth in our world.

His grey parents had left him
Mysteriously and rapidly—
How else is a shark born?
They had bequeathed him the odor of blood,
And a sense half of anguish at being
Perpetually the forerunner of blood:

A desire to sleep in the currents fought
Against the strong enchaining links of hunger,
In shoals, or alone,

Cruising the white haze off Africa,
Bucked Gibraltar, rode into the Atlantic—
Diet of squid, pulps, a few sea-perch.

But what fish-sense the shark had
Died with his shadow. This commonplace
Of kicking legs he had never seen:
He was attracted. High above him
The sunsoaked heads were unaware of the shark—
He was something rising under their minds
You could not have told them about: grey thought
Beneath the fortnight's seaside spell—
A jagged effort to get at something painful.

He knew the path up was direct:
But the young shark was curious.
He dawdled awhile, circling like a bee
Above stems, cutting this new smell
From the water in shapes of fresh razors.
He wasn't even aware he would strike;
That triggered last thrust was beyond his edgy
Power to choose or predict. This
Was carefully to be savored first, as later
He'd get it, with expertise, and hit fast.

He knew he was alone.
He knew he could only snap off
A foot or a hand at a time—
And without fuss—for sharks and dogs
Do not like to share.
The taste for killing was not even pleasure to him.
And this was new:
This was not sea-flesh, but a kind
Of smoky scent of suntan oil and salt,

Hot blood and wet cloth. When he struck at it
He only grazed his snout,
And skulked away like a pickpocket—

Swerved, paused, turned on his side,
And cocked a round eye up at the dense
Thrashings of frightened spray his climb touched.

And the thrashing commotion moved
Fast as fire away, on the surface of sun.
The shark lay puzzling
In the calm water ten feet down,
As the top of his eye exploded above
Reef and sand, heading for the shallows.
Here was his time of choice—
Twisting, he thought himself round and round
In a slow circling of doubt,
Powerless to be shark, a spawned insult.

But while he was thinking, the sea ahead of him
Suddenly reddened; and black
Shapes with snouts of blunted knives
Swarmed past him and struck
At the bladder of sunlight, snapping at it.
The shark was blinded—
His vision came to him,
Shred by piece, bone by bone
And fragments of bone. Instinctively
His jaws widened to take these crumbs
Of blood from the bigger, experienced jaws,
Whose aim lay in their twice-his-length
Trust in the body and shadow as one
Mouthful of mastery, speed, and blood—

He learned this, when they came for him;
The young shark found his shadow again.
He learned his place among the weeds.

The Black Ox's Curved Back

Where is there true strength.
In my spine?
Not in my head, or in my heart.

Can stamina come from sleep?
My knuckles are tiny stones
That can be broken.

Over the grass the mosquito gobbles everything.
His proboscis firm, sharp
As an anesthetist's needle.

I welcome him. Sting here! Sting to the heart!

Cockroach and Star

The sea rises at night,
The white-walled village submerged in the sea-wind.
A cockroach gazes at a star,
Its feelers meditating death.

Nightmares rise with the sea.
White walls make the peace of asylums.
Cockroach and star

Are each unfathomable—
They are not my contemporaries.

To kill the one and gaze at the other
Traduces ideas of time and space
No equation solves. We're each his own
Night and nightmare toiling around one vine.

I look, and could have believed
All things my eyes held, gripped fast,
Were mine for life, without question.

I could have believed: but watch
The frantic energy of the dying cockroach
Feel towards a star which I thought
In rage my foot'd brought closer—
The average savage act of a man
Who by killing the small, achieves the great
By default; or thinks he does.

The whole night becomes that star.
In dreams the cockroach winds its milk-
White wound around my open mouth—
I roar, and darkness chokes the sound.

The Circle

The spider hasn't dreamed about his
Place in history; nor does the fly
Feel persecuted, churning around on its wings.

The spider's merely a grapple for his stomach;
The fly, trawling in muck

Talks too much for its own good.

Even a butterfly, a mouse, or a small bird
Falls to the bigger species of spider—
Mechanical like tanks, patient as machine-guns;

But the fly works no miracles.
Not like the ruly ant, or the self-
Sealed factory of a spider's nerves.

The naturalist has no allegiances: he watches
The beginning and end of the short, unequal tale
Again and again, until his notebook's filled;

And at night, their scale small and intact,
The flies and spiders stream from his brain …

Entering his wife's dream, they eat her alive.

Two Riders

Loose, tethered loose
This horse combs serenity with its eyes,
Though fly-troubled.
The bigger man dismounts,
Moves round the horse's rump into full shadow.
The smaller one basks under his broad hat,
Under the strong sun that wrinkles a desert horizon
And sets lizards thinking.

This scene I just imagine.
Why is it so important—
Why erase the hazardous energy of life with what's
Merely apparent in the mind—
This tethered horse, the two contradictory men,
Different in habit, endurance and build,
Circling the one animal heart?

The men do not know me.
The horse in repose is companionable
Only in this moment of fatigue and trust.
The men must continually forgive each other
Their differences: they share this horse forever.
Probably trusting the horse they trust each other.
They have only stopped to rest themselves
Briefly in my mind: they are welcome.

The world, as they pose now, cannot change them much;
The true sun blacken or desert them
Beyond either's endurance.
The horse is all heart—,
Its resting heart goes pounding on like hooves
Any moment to gallop the desert to sweat on its back,
And be stabled at nightfall.

From *A Christ of the Ice-Floes* (1966)

Love-Stones

The three-day blow
Had tossed the lakeshore to its knees—

I found two stones
Lying side by side, just
Touching,
White eggs the sand wouldn't hatch.

But the sun came worrying through clouds
And poured its warmth across the sand—

Not to despair, but to explore
Word against word
The long distance between
Two stones that touch

Without speech,
And at the touching point
A little heat

And after a thousand years
The two stones may be joined

And the sun be forced to modify
The new stone's shadow—

Imperceptibly; because
Witness to witness the legend of the stones
Dies and is reinherited,

Changed, retold
Through no necessity, but

That the stones existed,
That the stone exists.

A Christ of the Ice-Floes

To the trees at the waterline—
Birches, a few elms, a glove of willows, a thorn—
His footprints crushed the snow
And stopped, where the ice was still heavy,
The river's current tearing at its shelves.
Was he deluding himself? Coming here …
It was neither a time of questions nor
Of answers, this in-between season—
Man remaking himself in the image of March,
His testicles drawn in,
His penis shrunken. In the black mid-current
A family of mallards crashed the ice
And swam away downstream … He heard their talk,
Biting the wind, and behind him
The forest dripped, trees
Distilling to earth, roots, leaves,
The monotonous melting. "Father" he said, "father"—
Who had imagined, once, his colonies
Of steaming chimneys, earth-proud, God-fearing,
Complacent but watchful, ready now
At the thawing to welcome him home.
The trick was to go away and then return
Later, without promising when,
Without foresaying relief or hope of his kingdom's
Homecoming … He was the word,
They the deed: and the deed deserted by the word
Meant nothing to them: or meant

Too much for their memory of him to outlast his going
And return. They were able—
His people. Upriver his eyes swung
With the turning wind; he saw the big houses,
Shacks, mansions, boathouses, a length of beach,
And the ice-floes ducking downriver like drowned sheep
Or so many souls, in the mind,
Starved water, without fish rising ...
It was cold, this halfway season,
White, with the false purity of whites,
Wind-chafed skin, the brown earth breaking.
He'd come to imagine his future, not theirs;
He saw now the need of his coming was their myth,
Powerful as the strengthening of each season—
As inevitable, as unbelievable as the first
Bud or flake or brush of puberty—
He took up a stone near his feet
And shied it skittering over the drift ice ...
Its brief splash broke him awake ...
He felt the water forming round his ankles,
Swaying, rising ... he didn't know he was walking
Until the last ice gave, and he stood in the river,
As the stone'd stood—
Less than an instant—,
The brown hair vanished, and the thorn tree drowned.

Winter Homecoming

The airfield stretches its cantilever wings,
Its petrified flight of a gull ...
Time is before me, blown by the solar wind
Lit by the sun's corona on the snow-sheeted glass.

It is daybreak, heart of winter.
The big jets listen, waiting for their flights.
I watch the blue-veined snowfields bleed with sunrise

Slowly turning my hands to catch,
Reflect, the cold light; asking myself

The way
The messiah comes.

Painfully he comes. Comes now,
As beyond the grey, wolf-shy pineforest,
The ice-shy villas of Montreal,
A million mirrors turn their heads
Watching this bird of departure, hearing his roar
Eventually even to the cross on the mountaintop—

He shakes the blood-pink snowfields,
His red light … green light flashes over the whole
Snow-tortured North—

Touching the snowshoe hare, the arctic fox,
Alarming the businessman sleeping his whisky off …

And I am coming to you this last time
Before the spreading sun has touched your eyes,
Passed on, and left no dawn where your eyes were.

Catkins

One of a thousand dust-blown, touchy
Shrubs in high summer, the catkin in March

Is a nettle of veins in a white eyeball
Pricked red against the ghost birch-wood and flooded farmland.

Here, where the hills begin
Is catkin country. Up this old cart-road
Shaking our city springs, tumbling the windscreen
High and low, as if the car were a wounded

Bird trying to keep aloft of the flood—
The wiry, March-stiff catkin waits
Like fate for the open pen-knife—
The blade's squeak, the snap, and a branch of moth-soft buds.

We promised to bring her catkins,
Nothing else. But the cold that entered with us
Felt white, bloodless, in the hospital room. The furry buds
Would not stir. Our heat lay at their lost roots, and with hers.

Last Snow

The cold bottom pond
Lies black with a dog's hair of reeds and lily
Roots. The snow draws back from its edge like a hurt
Lip, grimacing … a winter twig
Pokes up, so stiff it could be strummed like wire.

Out of the grey sky, blueing in the west
An organ note is rising on the wind. Now March, slovenly
With its shag and rust-ice, responds, and the deepening note
Chords over the pond sending a rainstorm of ripples out

And around, leaving a last
Black licorice crease where the disturbed

Twig snags the tremor, and holds it …. I walk
Too close to the pond. I walk and do not reflect
What I walk around: not an eye, but a blind

Absence; a double white
Light in the western sky, and a light behind that light
Which comes with spring and revives the ice-sick earth
Sterile now with the woman's death whose birth was my birth.

And I look to the pond to decide for myself
(As in its depth it seems to become a decision)
Which way, and by what sign
Already known, and through what further nights when the skeleton shines
Time's ticking circle on my wrist,
I will come to own myself outright,
As the storm of this spring beginning owns the pond,
And the pond possesses the twig, which catches
This last ripple, and holds it, knife-still.

Meditation On a Pine-Cone

The pine-cone's whorled
Tongues; woody cavities opening red,
Stubbed, as they touch the air—
These rough hooked knuckles and deserted
Seed-rooms, after the long birth
And sudden drop—
Rain softens now. Rain brings peace over the grass.

II
Here is a city. The sprung cells
Released a people. Now the red money-spider

Hurries through empty rooms,
In and out the skulled eaves,
The firedamp walls. Here is a country—
Leveled with snow to the eye's last hope
And melting trickle. Beyond
Linger the tall parents, twitched by the wind's
Fired coals hissing in the rain …
Leaning out and leaning in,
The unattainable ancestry of the dead cone.

III

Say not dead. For in April, in May
The common blood-drop spider
(Glint of red on her body's globe
Where the sun lies coiled in thread)
Borrows this house for her children.

I pick this cone off the grass
And the mother is spilt. Through the dark
Snow-damp rooms her children
Seethe and panic over my hand—
Their ghostly nippers are sharp—
The cone bites back. The cone has another life now.

IV

In Pinecrest cemetery the wind
Snows prevailing north—
In summer it turns; it hums around the cone
And the cone's antennae veer and track the wind
Like a beating heart. The stones
Express their keep in names—
Whole families gathered around one tree
And the pathways glib with pebble-crush
And the mowers working circling swathes

On the green roof of the world where the cones lie—
Crouched cities glazed with webs in the morning-wet
And the name on this stone my own name
As if the cone's earth owned me too.

V

Not yet. Our feet climbed through grass
And cone-stubble to this burial-place—
Death, the quiet pivot.
At earth are the coils that draw me up with the wind,
The living mourners, grateful to live,
Keeping their better selves above the grave,
Burying the unmentionable deep, beyond false touch.

VI

But when the sun breaks through the rain
The drying cone whispers. Words are all you are,
Memory corrects the postures of your body,
Covers the mouth with a hand—
Words inhabit the sprung cone of my head, the cells'
Red spider-mites. And the cone has another life.

VII

I grope uphill and the wind pushes me back
Across a smoking front, breaking the grass like a sea …
I am numb, the cone is numb
In my coat pocket, numb but warm
In the weld of my fist. I carry you over the earth,
Your dwarf-hive a city, a tongued head
At the back of my heart. I carry you over the earth—
Though some would prefer
The adult tree rooted in its four seasons'
Confining coffin. We had no roots, ever—
Our fate was as the cone's I take in my hand,

Grafted to earth, to tree,
Dropping to grass: a pulse only,
Time-blown seeds sharing the wind with dust and rain,
The husk, the house, flung open to the spider-invader
Gnawing her red mark in my hand's possession,
Patient only when the will is buffeted and bleeds.

Self-Portrait at Ten

The whipped horse was lame. We'd cycled to town,
My aunt and myself. There, at a crossing
Lurched a ragpicker's cart and the lame horse
Dancing, as if crazed hornets flew
At its skin from all sides. The ragman's whip
Was old and broken, like the man
Himself, and the lame horse … And a crowd
Of tourists with melting cones silently
Melting away, quietly back to their cars.
We stopped by the horse. "Stop that!" my aunt
Shouted; and the short whip
Fell across our shadows, stroke by stroke
Scored over the dust the horse's nerves at our feet.
And I think it didn't matter then,
But now it matters: what shock kept horses tame
Yet with every nerve gone wild under the whip,
Its eyes bone double worlds of scalding white
In the sun and dust. And the nag's
Tameness reached me; and my aunt's voice
Crying "Stop that!" while my thumbs
Burned white on the cycle-grips, the whole sky
Waiting to burst and rain on the horse the cry in me.

Visit of the Son

This is the address. The number is unknown.
They said to come, there is no telephone.

The stairway is uncarpeted,
The nails show through—

Heavier than air and light
I pass the paint-scarred window on the

Landing: it looks to the south,
The grass below is green, without details,

Blade or ladybird. A cat strolls off,
Shuffling through leaves in the quiet before night.

If I turn my back on the scene,
I am lit from behind: my eyes trill on in the dark.

On the dark stair something waits;
I welcome what waits, though it be faceless.

Something, a spendthrift moment where all
Comes eagerly back to life—

Where parents have gone; where loves go.
And it is a hellish wasteful idling plight

To be caught here, in one's time
Of own reflection, motionless as a stag!

How often the future seems to be
A green, prehistoric jungle at dawn ...

This, on waking: though the rain outside,
The lawn, the window looking south, they cheat me.

At the turn of the landing I stand,
Eaten by my own offense.

Say this is the end? But do not lie:
Say this is fate.

Say anything calm, counseled, trite and worn
So I may fight and be myself again.

Say … extinction. But the dust
I breathe is air, beneath this door.

Say I walk where the axis spins
And cannot keep my footing in the whirl.

Say nothing: the door is opening,
A freakish, spinning wind. White walls, and silence.

Such vigor in empty space!
Two lived here once—

Two lives. Two tongues have spoken
Words no other mind could know.

Supersonic dust! I shrug
These voices off, and prowl with the stride of a king

Over their floors of white air. In the glass
I touch my beginnings of a face, and grin.

Diamonds

Every man
Carries a scandal
At his heart.

The woodpile hides
A baby, or
A dead wife's bones.

In an ice-house down by the lake
On the damp sawdust, a coffin holds
The baker who went out hunting "to steady his nerves."

Nature a memory now—
Don't raise wild sap in a frivolous tree.
The land will not remember,
Or the sand, or the old stockbroker
Who drank his last martini in the lake one autumn night.

Leaves shake in the dust
Along the summer roads;
A cow gives birth to her calf, the world
Goes slack. Blood dries on the tines of straw.

And hay-stalks whistle through the field
Where a rusted car, its glass knocked out
Moans in the sun beside a plough,
A lesser ribcage, half-buried.

The pineforest
Heavy with dinosaurs—
In their depth the black is moving—

Blueberry bushes in the scrub

Stained our pails and fingers,
Boy, girl, and the breath of the blue juice.

And later the dirt,
Outhouse, hole of a mother skunk,
A prickle of flies and disease, streaming over the lake
To spider islands ...

We killed a crow by the rainbarrel,
Peppered it with B-B shot.
Three nights the crow slept in my bed,
The fourth day I took and broke my gun.

Later I made amends—
My mind the temper of the lake
Changing like the color of an eye,
Or rooted: an Algonquin burial mound
Whose hair of cedar hides the old scalp wound.

In the slow fall of needles
Two old pines
Remembered they were man and wife.

Faded blueflower curtains,
Pinewood walls,
Pimples plucked by flashlight in the mirror—

This house was my body once,
My first two skins, water and wind.

Now shadflies go the way of salt
Over a shoulder, through the pores of screens.

Such delicacy as I caught
In the nighthawk's cry, the kindred

Whip-poor-will, like the cry of a young tree

In its growth …
The nail is in the tree's heart,
Hammered home with the flat of a shoe.

The house is up for auction soon.
Small fish turn tail and plunge through the pools of oil
To fresher waters.

I,
Down the same darkness,
Retrieve my lost diamond.

Either/Or

I
    you
         witnesses—

the doors between us   glass doors
through the clothes and skin
                  and the senses'
      circuit
from event to event
               are interlocking circles
      never concentric
never the same wound in the same place
      but a shift in the air
like a mouth riding alone   through the spaces
      of rooms: speaking
whisper-cautions   less than that   lip-readings

There is no vanishing-point
                           between people
where either is the other, one is both
                           and the crime is single—
          no betrayal
     only the mouths of each
for whom the same words have bone-different meanings

As in this rest-house
high in the Shan mountains
watching the fire die down
which our hands built like a house

I fret for the future   but am at peace in the now
                           and no new thing
                      can blend us or divide us
          beyond what we are
and will be.

Dirge

The train all night dappling lights in the edge of our eyes,
Country lights, lonely fevers of the solitary sick, or bringing
Cities alongside: as if the stationary earth
Were traveling, and not us, dropping behind, like a litter of jewels
Left by an aristocracy … an empty throne
Whose debased queen you are. And I am flying north
To the sea-grey silence of dawn below the Scottish border—
Sleepless, rheumatic in the night wind—
Who can tell where we wake at the night's end?
I think of the stars, but I see only lights
Giddying behind; lights, and the stamp of the axe

That has hewn down forests, leaving only feasible stretches
Of houses, with lights in one window …
Your mind, sleepless, lit, over a cooling coffee cup
Nodding me on: north, north, the shale-grey nursing sea.
Do I go on forever, or do I return to you
Solid and strong as the black paunch of an oak
Whose crown, somewhere out there under the stars
Receives the wind, like lies, like truth in the willing ear
And always in darkness? By day
I will have lost these measures, and their signs—
I will litter myself with whisky; I will be
Abominable even to the organist of my far youth
Whose deep, held note, in the train's black traction
Moans with the memory of waves breaking.
… I will wake with the cold sea surrounding me.
I will frown, think twice, and go south again, willingly;
I cannot promise what I will bring back with me,
Smelling of ether and surf, and a dawn that is raining with salt
Over the pebbled littoral where waves crave to touch, and wallow back
Into the timeless swallowing source, the grey burden of waking.

Construction Site

The slow work-gang
in donkey jackets
flounders in the
rubble, rescuing this place
from its Victorian shape and smell.

White powders fly
like bone-dust into the ether,
their silk breath

smothers a yellow tractor ...
dust is the scar's poultice. The men
breathe easily.

I breathe the dust, and am glad
the past is past.
I know not what I destroy
either; I only know that this dust
infects me with a terror of death—
that the serge-rough shadows woken in these stones
were tumors, bitter enemies of my time.

But as the red crane dips,
and the iron ball swings out on its clumsy wrist
to drub those old walls down,
I see: not a man, or a woman or child
but a white-faced television screen
smiling and boasting its ownership here with the stars—
and I am aware
no death or choice is final,
or time better than now.

Wherever Men Have Been

Wherever men have been, this
Snail-luster trail of scent remains permanent.
The wild animals test
Their lives against it; the spoilt forests
Remember a fugitive dream of shadows
Cautious and as slow as the rise of sap,
A muttering of herds, the first
Tentative fires. The sea remembers

A thrill of keels, the feel of an outgoing ship
And the slower complacent homecomings—
Wives widowed, the hominy fields and hill
Made fertile by the burial of a fish.
The trail winds round and round—
Other trails cross it: hot at the touch of a nose
It blazes briefly, is torn in the brain of the tiger
And leaps rivers; and if one
Stumbles and drowns and drifts back to the sea,
Their mourning is brief as shock,
And the trail continues. Withered arm,
Withered eye—
The spearman's blunderbuss and the hunter's bombs
Disrupt little: the earth resettles—
Broken cities, books burnt,
Blood-trail leading nowhere but a patch to die alone in,
Winding, winding round,
Carrion of the quick mistake,
Ill-luck and the mastery of gunfire—
Till the monsters become flesh,
And the trail grows claws and follows on its belly,
Footsteps ghostly following through the elephant grass
To where sewer-grilles breathe
Gases and mice in the face of a waiting cat.
Don't turn now, don't look back—
Is there a need to know more than they know
Already, where the feet have walked,
Crawled, or run ... where the circle of sick slaves
Waited for death as a dying man waits for God?
Nerves, flies ... the brain eats through its skull,
An acetylene impulse sears the stomach away
And the trail quickens. Where are their inventions?
Don't ask now, don't look back—

A ticket will take you farther than you know.
One by one the animals leave the earth
And the trail goes broad and deserted ...
What are they to you but the tenants now
Of a fiery disillusion? Wherever men go to,
Not like the elephants or the slaves to their last
Glade, those mammoth hills of skulls
Discovered, and the scrambled tusks and hoofs,
Earth doesn't answer, the noises don't answer.
The frigidaire hums its song to the North Pole,
And one bleak outcast dog answers, howling ...
Years and years and years—
The rusk-whisper of grass at heel,
The binding vision of the first man born.

From *Firebreak* (1971)

Poem

A year
burning away time.

Where are the words?

The room
was full of people,
but they didn't speak.

A year
without love or hate—

no natural
cleansing or disfigurement—

lying awake,
watching the car lights play
and the branched wind wash the walls, until life

is another form of time
without substance, breathing.

America.
One more rash of lights
in an interminable orbit. Round

and round,
the earth, the moon—

praying for that innocence now
which must keep talking,

or stops forever.

Taos

Hills become trees

horses become trees

the wind whickers,   a chestnut
colt, caught
                in the barbwire

as the men
ride the mare away   uphill

Texas Spring

Headlights in the mirror on a lonely road
frost-still in the warm moonlight

I begin to wonder who my killer is
crawling through deep, dry sand in the craters of
                                    my footsteps

on a bottom of solid glass
                        skidding, searching past

the light-stabs
in the heart

No one, love
just distance
            The high beam with a warning light
and a horizon of dulled silver

where trees pray eternally to the winds
                                    lapping the sea at their roots

inland
so far from water
the engine sucking us on

As I am
and as you are
flesh a time-bomb, acorn packed with fire

weasels in their chimneys

solid beef digesting in the rancher's gut.

For Woodwinds

The dry wind ticks in the leaves
The coral snake has left his hole by the water pail
The days climb to a hush
oven noon, and at night
the hidden river leaves a lake in the cup of your belly
where
we dabble like children, lights out
to the small wild noises in the grass
and the dead eye of the gun in the bedside drawer

          II
Some mornings
the sea returns. Our valley of air
alive with sunshapes, shed scales
solders our lungs with the plumb pressure of tons
                                    of dark water

No life
 no appetite
But sap drips from the sun into our eyes
 staining the dust
The cardinal high in his tree
warns of the snake's return

 III
Juniper green on electric blue
enduring while the first leaves fall
and the road subliminal, grey
grainy film of a dead river, goat bones, glass
glitters through dust
 More dead
and many wounded. They cry for time
to tell us what to live for, not to die for—
the old who would take us with them over the river,
lacking the blood we drown in.

A Beginning

First this house
it is not mine
it has no roof
it has no walls

the house is just a frame

I lie where the winds blow across me

Second, the land
I do not own it

east west and south
canyon and snow mountains

to the north a sloping field

I walk where I am the only hunger

Thirdly, yourself
I possess but do not
possess
        animal
slow as the seasons
caught in the long count of the blood

we roof the house
we nail the walls

we walk in the company of our shadows

Three

I have known three healers
    one, a dead woman
    nearer than anyone
she left to inhabit a tree, under
         the snow I will not meet her
not now

Another was a man
      a greying haired child
    whose vanities were small, his love
a need of love
      bewildered by the world

he loved and feared

You are the third, the one of pure chance
        my wife
                by being no more
than you are. May autumn and the night
                        winds cool your fever, now
quiet house
                green blanket
sleep.

Nocturnes

The lake's banked fires
hiss at the water brim

Words spoken at dusk
                        still echo
nothing wilder than fish

Only the cricket stirs
a warning in the reed-beds

footsteps of a ghost

        II
Calm after the accident the cars
melt in the crimson siren
of blood
        Between its stone cliffs
bent like a broken bone

the road lingers, watching

the pine trees tilt their faces at the stars

III

I dream of the coral snake
and you, your body in its Indian silence

brushed by grass
the sweet green stain

padding over stones
hand in hand, towards the dark river
                              the hidden moon

Memorial II

I visited your grave
too often in dreams
while you were still alive

Now I do not want to touch
the real body and the real grass
see the real trees

              Because
your voice will begin to describe
the leaves, the ladybugs
roots as they are
                    the germ of wind
that reaches you
flowers, your neighbors' names

the same voice
that claimed and exclaimed so often

such things, your eyes
                    quicker than mine
                        still quicker than mine

X4

Fell into a false sleep—woke up
there were clouds smoking across the stars
white clouds

and a wind in the room
the room alert, the curtains alive
in their night-dance

My northern friend, asleep by the East River
My southern friend, asleep by the lake of mountains

No one comes,
no one goes

            II
The crisis is to tell it as it
happened, before it escapes
                —the news of her death,
and of a new love come, my water-bearer,
time beginning

So little the self
so crude
            without much love or pity

The sea goes deeper than the soul
She is one of the sea's voices, having met no soul

worth living for

And you, what can I tell you?
The wind blows through your sleep
You dream proverbial dreams

We are now

III
The moon in her first quarter gone and the wind
now overcast

hidden nostrils, sleeping fingers
hair at a toss on half-pillows
                    bedroom smells

the slow death and the slow birth of cells
seepage of time; no wonder dreams

fail us, no
telling the true figures the dead left

IV
I repaired the burnt-out room at last
covered the charred rafters with
asbestos sheet and a gallon of white paint

a bed and a rush mat
two chairs, a desk, a bookcase
keep it simple—

the sun by day, the wind by night
reviving the dead-world. Your long journey through the dark
never ends, clock

no count, silver and black
the great circle wheels through the stars—

our words leave shadows where they fall.

Lament

She chose
the sun for myth
in a land where snowdrops thrive
on cold and water,

fine bones
showing the skull,
leaf-skeleton
longer than any summer:

one would not know
how fine her waiting, her
sorrow, the gestures of life
kept to the end

October

You dream about circuses, the clown, the tightrope walker,
heights, and falls, drums and horns,
sequined bareback riders,
ringmasters with whips
                         the smoky tent
of autumn, nights

of dim lamps and sawdust, tumblers and acrobats
circling you, through fiery hoops
                              putting you through your paces,
glare-red eyes,
at whip-touch,
                and the dead faces
                        under the great cone of smoke
applaud you
or jeer you—
you are one unlisted, your act begins in silence
you wait for the end of night, biding your time
                                        their attention
desperately, yours,
                    for the sun to rise,
sorcery of the will, for the sun to rise
burning out the canvas sky, cone
                              of smoke, dim light—
for theirs is another age
a time before sunrise
and you must see them die in the great fire of your will
                              under the hooves
of the scared beasts
you have started—

to begin at sunrise imitating the birds
to lie under the leaves that hide the stars

Sickness

You turn
in the green circle of fever
at grass

               above your grave
beneath the sun

between
ice-age and tropic
talking new life into the earth
                    burn and cool

dancing in the moon
the hot evening star
            and the cooler star of morning
murmurs

of cold sea
the sweat-bed ocean sand
where the drowned airman lay wrapped
                        in his parachute
eyes on the hidden stars

two hundred feet of darkness

there, for a time
mollusk
to your revival and play in the dry
                winds of Wyoming
shell-beds, hills

I wait for your journey to end
for the sun to draw your poisons

we who have no gods but keep returning.

From a Yoruba Poem

The light-beast rose early
stepped, like the duyker
"Shaking the grass like bells"

in the garden, by the water pail
where the coral snake lived
under stones soaked
by the dripping tap

euh! euh! the deaf-mute
deer-sound, so like a young goat
born in a dry-season ditch

I wish I could talk like that

spare word that needs no mirror
that does not dance for itself
but steps
"shaking the grass like bells"

in the heart of the hunter
who knows
what it is he must kill, preserve

of life
for life to return, rising early
to catch the light-beast in the grass
before his shadow crosses it

From *Where the Arrow Falls* (1974)

Part One (excerpts)

1

The top of your head is still open
fragile, hearing whispers of the sun

your teeth are early and strong
your birthmark grows
a rose, in the small of your back

your eyes are smoky and dark
the lashes longer than ours

your rage
knots you so
I can't untie you

all in all you're a fine one
your strength in Leo but jammed between
Aquarius and my fish

soon you'll be a year
our trees are full of owls
our chimney full of young swallows

fire and water and air
and the earth is yours to grow on

meanwhile you have no friends

8

At night or just before dawn
dogs in the valley
baying, up the loose stone road
              invaded our hill
a deer? light hoofs
broke the woods' edge
before the wild night mouths
              that broke my dream
melted to echo
the nightmare
              the blood chase
hungry, always hungry
and the bones of the hills glowed
in the afterlight
              the river
under a red unrisen sun
or a red unsetting moon
              in the small hours
when time returns
and the stone breasts of the hills
suckle the deer to their deaths
              or to mine: foretold by the heart's
hoofs leaping
the loose stone road
breaking the woods' edge—
deer-self, deer-self!
              ahead of the dogs
all windows open like eyes
              and the stars closed
knowing now
not archetype or dream

but the breaking lungs and heart—
and the forest alone is safe—the forest alone!

10

There is no equality among those
who suffer. Tones come through
into the bones of the ear, we

hear crying, the
depth of the crying is unknown but
as light changes, we feel it:
the light before rain

     the light after rain

Love
can not redeem this. Torn
from its light, the eye knows nothing but pain,
though the light is pain, you
could not touch the pain
in your daughter's eye but

find a jungle. Those
who must live, cannot live
easily. What breaking point—
when the sun spread its talons and fell
on her playroom: fire
feathers blood her father's eye

We must be
fanatics even to breathe. The
quiet ones more so. Cold

as the sharp-shinned moon over
the cedars. It
is alone.

13

As I grow older
I lose that fire
that left these scars,
new music in my ears

Now I dance for the sake of play
but be careful: this
too is a phase, old
matter can return … said

the goat who sang the mass
watching Goya paint
the last face, his hand
not broken like his mind

the bleating shadows
the bad breath of the starved
there is still a Duchess of Alba
A white pretender to God

14

As people dreamed
of shipwreck, now

planes crash nearby, in a mothlike flame
                          or owl wings: there
are never survivors

in a flight of five jets
one folded its wings
and fell

I woke with fire on my skin
it was dawn: a
                          swallow beat on the fire screen, black
and white of old ash. I
opened the door, it planed into the wind

and the young ones in the chimney
cried for food—
I am not milk or worms
                          your mother will come

but the air
seemed waiting: my eyes, winged with flame
flew over the trees
                          hunting for victims, heat
to body's heat, the soar
of ash settled to cloud
the sun did not rise

someone, somewhere, gone

my bed is a swamp, and I lie
draining into the lost bones under me

it is late and the world is old

in the word "beginning" I hear no end

16

Cottonmouth
dead
with a hole
in your side

flies at the closed mouth
flies at the hole

even now
I wouldn't touch you

olive, with rusty bands
the slit eye
only a picture of watching

broken *S*
shape in the stony dust
far from water, where your bite is worst
in death, venomous still
as ripped from the living

—Pilinzski, patient Hungarian
I have your papers on my desk

to try and bring you alive
this day the snake died
in this dust, Harbach
cripple

venom
in memories ... stones
of dry Texas, not

those dark potato fields
where prisoners crept

between wires hung with scorpions
and daybreak, the spirit's release

into no new world

20

Not Navajo
you don't count

not the child
of a Maya god
you have no name!

wanderer: where are the lives
you have put behind you

the mask
torn from your face
tears flesh with it

where in the whirl is the self
blood-of-bone, though you

may dance and speak
with tongues of the older dead
who are you? what

gift but your loss
do you bring

to the listeners
under
the hill—

Maya, Navajo
Yaqui, Hopi, Tlingit, etcetera

those sleepers
deep
beneath your fjords and farms

your city's
secret arrowhead

its closed
bloody
eye

26

autumn in spring

      what does happen after
a long night: of
cities we cannot repair again, dark
roads, red rivers
      the Cheyenne stumbling north
through autumn blizzards
dead as the figures on cards
      kings, and queens

what does
happen to the mind

waking in cloud
burned by dreams, no
less self than the wary deft-
handed body gardening stones
           this Wednesday, the sun
a fiery negative

come mask
and be the season you pretend
our lives
are photographs we cannot burn

let heroes
know who they are, their
false selves wake them at night
to find no new image in the
           horror that killed a people, no
dead tongue, no living dream

I rode the horse into spring
the cloud and thunder mare
           with a lame leg
but the hills were autumn, autumn brown
there was no fear and no pain

but I imagined I was alive again

29

He asks each sunrise
for a new mask
to be worn until his

face can take the sun

        habit, habit
gone in the nights
lost, like dogs
so the fumbling of his hands
savages things

even
when light
is clearest—

this black one hangs in the hall
it is a gift, like his others

no one
completes its phase: they
      grow inward and vanish, crying
names
he cannot give them: they
want someone, are mates of light
weeping elsewhere

     ii
       they are a crowd
come to no
event, random
as a leaf pile

dark faces of a Sicilian funeral
bright faces on the Padre Island sand
conning shells
this
stalling of the mind—

why will he not choose one
and wear it?

iii

By noon the number of the day
is a continuous thunder,
the black mask has no body
but has become what it can see
inward, and trees,
cedars, circle the wooden shed
waiting for the cry "Eureka!" or "Fire"
to come as the wind climbs
                        higher and higher

and sun
crawls the cliff
like diamondbacks ... the
unrepentant rocks are his bones too
his back bends with the river
old fishbones put on flesh
and dance his eyes two circles
the holes in the middle are night
his mouth is a widening song

one by one
his fingers put out leaves, searching
for airs they have not touched ... this
is where Hamlet falls
where Little Wolf shot Thin Elk through the heart

iv

the last is human
to bear the blood of others
through the mask's eyes

where no holes were carved

to give or take
pain

        "in my life
too little compassion"
            —his father

what then

comes of knowing his trees
more faithful than friends
his animals
less so

        the mask is mad
its madness is black, it
grips night and shakes it

it is hungry for the face it hides

    v
at night came the storm
at daybreak the shaken rocks
hung loose from matted holes
there was smoke on the wind
a glitter in the grass

he cried for the mask to come
and touch him to his feet
five fingers climbed his backbone, hooves
of elk multiplying
expert at silence

where were the caves of the storm
hiding, a
city aware of its end, an
iron bridge no longer above its river, the
mask's eyes, black lava

wept centuries too far back
old smoke, old fires, old rain
she touched him with these fingers
he got up dragging her hand
to the fire and held it there

       vi
his trouble
his having no face

his having eyes

but no face

like anything that watches
is unknown, whole

of the whole earth
but nothing, mask

speak to her kindly
and not of the stars

his soul is a clam
in a borrowed shell

by night
the faces have gone

his true face multiplies through all
the deaths it comes to

asking, asking
to be seen

as God
was once

in a
corn seed

32

Then comes the screaming dog
his tail on fire   face
of my father   over the grass he
sets smoking

it is dark   his body
lies burning where it fell   Trees
kneel over the grass
mound   I am a child
looking   I see
grass but no fire no body no dog no face

       ii
Sure, sure he was here
right there! You can hear the wind
a mile away from the top of the valley, vultures
brush the treetops, wind
comes home

                              This picture
needs a woman. Brown
weed in the day-green water, river
asking the cliff for more sun

cold, cold water

          iii
And he has become
the thin tail of the fish. Who
kept me half my life is now my child

She? are both one eye
his hazel mixed with her blue
that is the river color running
through limestone

                         … fiery dog

you burnt me

it is dark
trees bend to the river listening

no grass no fire no body no dog no face

36 (excerpt)

          ii
A prayer before a journey

the painted desert touch
our pale skin with its colors

the mountains lift their horns
they smell us coming

we are inert: the world moves

      iii
behind us we leave
rivers bouldered with dead

in the rising sun it is their blood
that drowns us

in the rising wind their voices
make us listen

forked tongue of snake and rifle
morpheus of polaroid eyes

probes for the hole in the heart

      v
I say good night to all the creatures of fear
they will return

my pale skin takes color from the rocks
I am dressed in splendor

leave me. I know this desert
I turn my red heart out to the pale mountains

I walk in the sun

39

Juniper you stand in the west wind
dry old man of the high plains

so dry
the air is fire
so old
half of you is dead

holes in you the birds have pecked
like dead eyes
gnarled against the weather
your hair falls at a touch

you were our only shade
you stopped what little wind you could

we spoke to you in the night
our closest neighbor
the moon took on
your shadow from the sun

now it is time to go

I touch you like a son
your dry white flank
knows nothing but heat cold wind
father tree

now you are alone in our eye
now you are alone on the land

our dust flies east to cities

41

I see a face in the stone
because you say
there is a face in the stone

also I saw
an angel in her, because
she said: there is an angel in me

and I willed it

now there is nothing but
a memory of a face and an angel
this hot morning
without wind

ii

Last night they shot me
but I got up
and ran to a lake
but the lake was dry

I passed a pony
running thirsty
he had a red wound
on his flank, from the sun

he whinnied, he
thought I had four legs
the lake was a dry red bed
I do not know where the water had gone

iii
This is a country
of deep lies
the face in the stone, the angel
the pony, the dry lake

but the wound
bled, I
feel it today in the sun

and the voice of the pony
mistaking me for its kind, the
wound in me, the
wound in its flank, was bleeding

iv
I do not know who was shooting
who drank the lake dry who
carved the stone who
made her an angel

but
there is time to learn
why I came to this place, why
I was running, and who were the others

I cried to warn
not to come closer
not to come closer

my tail was on fire and my mane

46

These elegies, black dreams
I can't unknot their names
I put my head in their mouths
bite out their tongues
but they speak

night after night
wings of the condor, whistling from high snow
slashing the dead graves
open

dear ones
he did not know
earn or love to the limit of him, what
cried in his sleep was not birds

his ghost-shirt caught in a tree
he smacked the air with his hands
the voices talked him under

let him begin now
give him his daily bread

Part Two

1

I have built you
nothing, what
have I given

distance,
no rest

      no rest
but movement, coming
and going
like the south clouds, over the valley

your eyes

you are waiting for me
but I am here

I think

2

Round and round
the rooms, padding
      on quiet feet

on bed
with your book and bolster, reading
the weather and Lawrence

our nerves make love, we
tear like webs

burn in the late day sun

things here
and absent

3

Quiet as stones, but
unable to weather as stones

our skins
are in love

the crazy jagged colors
of bad dreams, time
gone to the lost, hurt, hunted
ones behind us

there are few
who have stared at the sun
and kept their eyes

mine
or yours

4

Sometimes
the body a god
      sometimes water

sometimes
the eye
its lifetime back through dark

the entrails
congealed in the eye's
      beauty, watching

all that is there
inside and out,
bird complete in its song

but afraid
to fly

5

It is quiet here
no one comes

we wear clothes
for the trees and birds
      not for each other

why then
what do we hide

does blood
show secrets through the skin

or do our soft parts
go masked
          like a god
to keep their power

pure and hidden?

6

When your eye
is in me, I
break

you take
the pieces and
build me a body, no

one I know yet

your lover
my stranger

our child

7

It was so long
and the night

filled with dead faces, crying
to be alive

I found you
in the moon's grave, about four,
some fire you had dreamed
which the black cedars witnessed, kissed

on your body, a live scar
that burned my side

and you
can never tell me

8

We find our selves
as children, but

the masks we wear
come as man and woman

to touch. The child
fades from our eyes

returns as one
who does not know us yet

but in her
the masks will die

a child will return
to both our eyes

9

It is liveliest to be still
listening to some things come and others die

now, when our wills are quiet
breathe as the trees do, without fear

not hidden from man or sun

10

I have built you
nothing, but
our cells know a difference in winds

in touch
a danger

I prayed
to a warped cross, now
I stand half broken, heal me

our cells will melt and close

now is the sun, our moment, given, whole

11

To see it all fresh
forget

bury the bones
then try and find them

hard
harder than death

I am afraid of innocence and
I cannot remember, night
my duty to dream

smells of the wet cedar

my book reads itself
my house is watching me

music out there: rock of the storm
home has eyes
            wind smells of cities
you

forgotten things
drift up in the light
fish-heads without bodies
with living eyes

my duty to dream, not sleep, not
ease like a snake into the hole
of knowing, without eyes

and you are watching
your skin is a number of years
a song I know and don't own

a poem to be found

12

Between midnight and daybreak
seven times for my sins
staring the different winds into their cradles
            owls, nightbirds, cats
the faces I know and do not know—

betrayed by my silence
I think of you now: you burn with me
in this foresleep, before taking your masks and roles
into dreams I cannot control, where
            you triumph or die—
and leave me a husk clinging to a tree

I imagine a better world, larger
a place where the hurt
smile over each others' cradles: dwarf, giant
            twins, the without arms or legs
ones, fat lady and rubber man, Ralph
the man with elephants' legs, the bearded lady—
a family circled by fire
but spared by the other-killing fire

so my head will empty itself
for its own sounds to enter:
the Fool coming late to his hands, an effigy
            of dried shit and straw, that
walks, talks, composes poems
that enter through one eye and out the other
so, in a perpetual circle

adobe man, lost on his own plains
a miracle of nightly resurrection and

daily sleep: Wakdjungkaga, between one birth
            and another, eating his own body, his
night confused with his day: no
enemies, no friends, no god but error

as even the stones   fitted to one another

From *Casual Ties* (1983)

They That Hunt You

They that hunt you know two things about you: your location and your name. Knowing your location, they can always find your name. Knowing your name, they can always locate you.

You are free to move about in the world as an unlocated name until your name locates you. You are free to stand still in the world as an unnamed location, until your location names you. Either of these might happen at any moment. They are not an either but a both.

Your change of name has not helped. Your change of location has got you nowhere. You are still what you are and will be taxed as such. Your long list of unpaid parking fines will spell out your name, retrospectively, and point to where you are this very moment. The children you leave behind you, if any, will lead them to the door you think you closed forever, the house whose number you changed at night when you thought no one was watching. Your lost mail has your name and knows where to find you.

This is the law. You are your own law, but this is *the* law. The law is the mask of the god with eyes but no other features. The eyes are empty. The eyes require your eyes to make them see. The sightless mask is hunting your eyes even now. Give, give generously.

It is for your own good. Your good is their goodness, you will be rewarded. You will be allowed, at times, to wear their mask, to fill its empty eyes with your eyes, to hunt for others as they hunt for you. The feeling of power, though occasional, will make it seem worthwhile. In between the times of power you can laugh, dance, sing, and play the fool you are. They are responsible and will take care of the others. You have no need to feel afraid. Fear is what brought you to this. Now you are cured.

Smile then. Exercise yourself in contentment. You are neither still nor moving, nameless or named. Your name and whereabouts are known to them who possess them by right. They are on loan to you until the time comes to recall them and reassign them to another who even now is being prepared to assume your name and place, your fear and ecstasy, your dread of living and dying.

Love him as you love yourself. Love them who made this possible. Love is generous. Love is to give to the hunter what he asks. Be freed by this. Go forth, be glad, and multiply.

The Big List

The other day a scrap of paper crawled in my direction, wanting an immediate answer. I said, what answer can I give, I only live here. It said, your life is at stake, your life is the answer I know already, which you are reluctant to give me. Paper, I said, in that case, go and give the answer you know already to whoever sent you, why bother me? The answer might be wrong, said the paper. Also, it must come from you, to show you are alive and not just a name on the big list. What is the big list, I asked. It is the record of all that has ever happened, said the paper, and I am its messenger. The answer is long, I said, it is very long. Are you sure you are big enough to carry it? The answer is in point form, said the paper. It must be short, very short, so that the big list does not become a nightmare of proliferating details, making you seem more important than you are. Your answer must make you look like all the others, but not so much like the others that you cannot be distinguished from their answers. Scrap of paper, I said, get fucked. That will do for length, said the paper. But as for content, it is extremely prejudicial to your case. The big list is serious. It is so serious it never smiles. Scrap of paper, I said, why are we playing this game? The answer you already have is the one the big list sent to you for me to repeat. Why invent another? The big list needs help, it said. The big list has been crying all day at its desk waiting for you to respond. Are you trying to tell me the big list has feelings, I said, it actually cares? No, said the scrap of paper, the big list hasn't a care in the world. But it is incomplete without your answer, it is *big-minus-one*, which is the sort of negative attitude it cannot tolerate. Help the big list. Help to make it whole. Paper, I said again, give the big list the answer you have already, the answer it knows. I will, said the scrap of paper. The answer is, you are dead. You are dead and your name will be erased from the list. Then the big list will be complete again. The big list will be complete and you will be dead. I will tell the big list that. Yes, I will tell the big list. Now crumple me up in a ball and throw me in your wastebasket. Say I couldn't find you. Say you never saw me before in your life.

Birthday

I walk backward into the time it takes to become my body. There are incidents here I can only imagine now: a gun left lying on a library table, no one there, the air filled with words read or left unopened. The journey in quest of the Grail is now a journey in search of a murderer who might be one of you. If the victim could speak he would say, I did it; open me, the words, the evidence, are there to read.

It was always my intention to create a riddle of what I am, to express it or suppress it, as I have done. Someone else will get into trouble for this. It is my way of involving you, or one of you, in my body which you have disowned, calling it not your own.

A little further on down the table, there is a pile of books. Two are empty notebooks. The other two are books, and I have written one of them: I leave you to guess which. One window has been left open, to suggest I left that way: exited, as they say now, putting the stress on a written word you see above doors, rather than the body that passed through the door. I can't imagine what these clues will mean to you.

I am in this empty library and am part of its emptiness: invisible, but continually whispering to you, through a thousand closed covers on the shelves. You look at those covers and you feel despair. Where do you start, which book do you take down? Because every start is a commitment, however mistaken. And as you begin reading, one after another, at random, a pattern will begin to form around you, a body, which is not your own.

It will develop a head, arms, legs, genitals, blood, lymph, organs, skin, and a hand will reach out from it and take the gun. The gun might be empty, like the two notebooks. Or it might be loaded, like the two books, one of which I wrote myself.

It is not my purpose to help you. The fact that neither of us is here makes me think we are looking for each other: or for another who doesn't exist, or is a hand reaching for a gun. Who is going to fill the empty notebooks? Who is going to read the unopened books? Someone will have to close the open window and turn out the lights.

I walk backward into the time it takes to become my body. The door closes in front of me, I walk away, and someone goes in. I try and stop him but it is too late, I am walking away. I cannot return now to see who was curious, or who was simply mistaken and chose the wrong door.

I am far away now. I hear a shot, and feel a burning in my stomach. Someone comes running towards me, bleeding and clutching his stomach. We collide, we fall together, and there is nothing there.

Being Absent

Where I am not is what begins to happen. I am a master of conclusions, sitting where I am, a receiver of accomplished facts, products, whose beginnings are beyond me. That girl who was married yesterday is not born yet. On an assembly line in Detroit, someone drops a wrench onto sheet metal. That sound comes to me as a poem, will come to me as a poem, when I hear it. This is the power you notice in someone who is not all there. It is not a power but a being absent: a remotion of essential particles, waiting to leap together at the sound of a word.

The word could be any word. The annunciation could be any moment. A dream reveals itself in the strange way someone begins behaving when you say: "cobalt." He might begin to mutter: "color, mineral, mother, sky" and break out in a sweat as if from cancer remembered or anticipated. This doll has lost an eye, and the eye was blue. The child no longer remembers the eye: it is a one-eyed doll and always was. Blue eyes got married yesterday. What color will our child's eyes be? The Polish worker in Detroit picks up his wrench and remembers how blue the sky looked over ruined Warsaw. The word is out of control. What begins to happen does not take place.

A kitten is dying again on the back porch. Several kittens have died this year, we don't know why. They become wobbly, torpid, unable to feed or move: they die in tiny convulsions with their heads stretched up and back. Something in their mother or the place is transmitted to them, or fails to be transmitted, and they die. The word is an antigen or a germ. Its beginning is beyond me, but its end is at my feet. I say, there is nothing I can do; but the word "do" becomes part of this sentence: the thing is done. It is a sentence of death. The sentence of a witness to the end who is not there when the event begins to happen.

The world is crying for milk. It is time to feed. It is raining and the smell of food is everywhere, it breathes out of the earth, in waves, convulsions, spasms. Food of life, food of death, food of word. Word as it comes to you long ago formed from its conception, whose witness you are, to use or not at will, to recreate a pattern that has ended or might end with you, in your hands, in the syllable you set yourself to find: a heartbeat weak or strong, beginning, continuing, waiting for its end.

Where I am not is what ceases to happen at last.

Telephone

Too early yet to tell what the day will bring.

But the nerves you get up with are what make things happen. They cannot be soothed or fooled. What am I to accomplish, asked the man eating a meager breakfast of toast. This is a day like any other. I am not a bureaucrat, but they have my number. Any moment now there will be a phone call. Something urgent has happened in my absence which requires my absence to pretend it is there. Resist, I tell my mirror. But my mirror is my number already being dialed. It has located my reflection: which is what they were waiting for.

Too late, the man steps back and hides his face in his hands. In the dark of his hands there is a landscape filled with night: rivers and red sandstone cliffs, where stunted people move about, with implements and goats, among tiny fires. For a second or two he watches them. There's a shout. He has been seen. They are coming for him with spears, running up the cliffs of his shut hands towards his eyes. The hands drop. His reflection receives him back. The phone rings.

He does not answer the phone. The phone rings. He does not answer the phone. The phone begins to talk. It rehearses his childhood, his life. Number by number it recounts his innumerable lives: cell after cell responds as it is called, remembered. He is summoned now to go to the source of the call: the phone's reflection at the other end of the long wire, where someone sits with growing patience, telling the lengthening story to which he listens, ring after ring, of the one who must eventually be present, whose life will have preceded him to this place where it is already recorded.

Who is about to enter the door now.

Talking

At a time when people still talk about the heart, where have the buffalo gone? I am driving beyond the sound of my own name. I am out here on the highway where the maps are older than the places I come to: always a strange turning that wasn't there, a settlement beginning to grow old as I speed past it, so that the girl of seven playing on her lawn where the settlement begins is that grandmother rocking on her porch at the other end, in a house grown much older, a frame house which had been a ranch-style bungalow with a TV aerial above it as big as a tree, allowing the girl of seven to look at any program she chooses, swept in invisible gusts, like the buffalo, like the wind, across the high plains and into our hearts, a dream which people still talk about as they talk about having a home, whether they are seven or seventy: a heart, a home.

My car is insane, and I must keep talking to it, keep it moving. The way I talk to my car is the way I would talk to my home, if I had one, narrating the way it must keep changing, adding to its mileage or its number of rooms, as its lifeline grows, its family increases, without a break: for to break the story of journey or settlement would stop the heart for the instant it takes death to enter and wreck the car or reclaim the home. We are married and must grow old together. If we fail to grow old we have not lived. We have not passed through that settlement where age happens at once, so suddenly that the settlement is not on our maps before we come to it and not there after we have left. So I keep talking to my car. My life depends upon the words I choose.

I myself am of indeterminate age and avoid mirrors. All, that is, except my driving mirror, which reflects my eyes from time to time as I glance at it: the eyes that never change and appear to be looking backwards even as the highway draws them forward along an infinite thread of grey or black converging at some point never reached, in memory's other space, where give me a home where the buffalo roam is the nursery song I was raised on, heard again in the speed of this car, the stillness of this house. For I am very still sitting here in this vinyl rocking chair, the wheel in my hands, thinking how old I have grown with my house, how young I am about to become when I reach that settlement, where my seven year old bride waits playing on her lawn and settles her walking stick between her legs, in a print dress, peering over her spectacles at a fine line of dust that could be my arrival or my departure. If I can just keep talking it will be all right. I must nurse this thing to a point where I feel I am neither moving nor still: where the map, my heart, fills slowly with the ghosts of unborn buffalo, whose song is the wind beating against my house, buffeting my car with words I haven't found and names of settlements which are born and die as a child's ball rolls into the street and stops.

The Text

One has been there and one has not. Two might have made it a place, an occasion, to remember. But two were not there: one had to invent the other, so the place and the occasion were fictitious, and what one saw truly with his eyes was his own falsehood, pleading with the wind, the waves, and the gulls to confirm his legend: as Odysseus' legend, lying open on his knees, was confirmed by the ocean, looking east, the early morning sun, at the place he had marked and left open, as if to attract what might come riding in on the waves of this more northern sea at the beginning of his day.

He writes one word in the margin: Open. He waits.

Stillness moves one. Movement holds one still. It is from movement that legends are born. It is in stillness that legends are written. The two make an occasion and a place. What is one up to, thinking he is thinking, unnerved by stillness, unable to move, sitting here at a place where the sun touches the sea, nakedly, without mind: waiting for something to open, for another to appear and call his name.

He closes the book on the word he had written, and waits.

One outwaits one's perfection. One waits and waits to be made incomplete. One is added to one, or one divides and grows: one becomes two, three, four, ten, and loses the godhood of the sun, and is everything under the sun, all things, all systems, all laws, but can never return: can never be that which never leaves itself and so never returns.

He opens the book and writes three words in the margin: Monad, Nomad, No-man. He waits.

The primal fire, from which all things come, to which all things return. He lights a cigarette and draws a circle in the margin. He touches the tip of the cigarette to the circle, and the circle burns, expands. Its black edge eats the words he had written, eats into the text of the sun, the beginning of his day, and stops for no reason at the O of Odysseus, whose journey is not yet complete, and therefore not fully begun: as one must know the end before he begins: the stillness in the movement of the heart.

He tears out the burnt page and waits.

Mummy, what is that man doing burning all the pages of his book and throwing them into the sea?

Ring of Bone

for Gary Snyder

Here we go, laughing. The way I saw it first made me think I had seen it getting killed, though it got up with a smile on its face and walked off, dusting the seat of its pants. "The pants are not the trousers," I thought to myself. "You can call the trousers the pants. But can you call the pants the trousers?"

I had coffee and thought about the difficulties we have with language. Beside me, a girl was hiccupping into her milk. I thought of my dog eating grass, and said, "Take her outside, she's going to be sick." But they said,

"Leave her alone. She's about to become a mother. Don't touch her or the child she bears will be deformed."

I have been on a hunger strike for seventeen days. It was like this all the time the hostage interviews were taking place, I couldn't eat, and whatever I tried to eat came up as propaganda and lies. I have been looking for a young mother with full breasts to help me out. But all I see are trousers walking, or call them pants, getting killed.

I wear my ring of bone around my left wrist and gnaw at it. I am teething again and the bone is as soft as rubber, but it tastes human. They tell me I am going feral. But I say, "No, I'm laughing." My laughter wears trousers and walks with a slight limp. I might adopt a child soon, or a young mother, but certainly not something I could kill by mistaking those words.

Tiger Tiger

The animal that thought itself a tiger scratched its eye out looking at the sun. A one-eyed tiger can still hunt, so this one thought of a smaller weaker creature it could chase and overcome, as its stomach felt hollow, and its mouth burnt from tasting too much breath and air.

That weaker animal ran ahead of it all day. It ran along the tunnel of the tiger's single eye, among the patterns of thought that dappled the floor of this jungle, skittering and flushing other game from the tiger's path, but never getting close to being caught. "This is a problem of perspective," thought the tiger, resting and rubbing its good eye. "I must think myself a second eye, in order to catch this creature I have thought escapes me."

That other eye rose with the moon, but it was blind. The eye was dead and white. It gave the tiger no pain, but it got him nowhere, as eyes go, as this one came. "When you ask for a gift," thought the tiger, "you must specify. Balefully I see that weaker creature stopped ahead of me, waiting for me to resume the chase. I have forgotten all else. I must think of something."

It thought the weaker creature moved. The tiger pounced and caught it, there was no struggle. It chewed, and what it chewed was a damaged eye, an eye that thought to itself as it was being swallowed down, "What insight on the tiger's part to see how close I was to him all the time."

A First Drawing

Brown before the first big spring rain, moot, lie the rangelands and meadows, scattered with patches of that coarse, tall, silvery grass whose name I'm always forgetting, which crawls partway up the low cropped cedar hills and stops before the rocks take over, making little cairns around the stuntier cedars, with a buzzard or several sailing around the summit to lend perspective. Now the heavy rains have come and the thin soil can't hold its nourishment, it spews in brown flood down the dry creek beds and through small towns and trailer camps that wake to brief nightmare, then shake themselves like a muddy dog and trot off, or get up, stretch, and rebuild. Morning fogs and night fogs. If someone drops a hammer in the valley the sound hits my foot: I wince, curse, turn on the light and look at the clock. It is always late and there is always a noise. I think of people I know lying in their beds and wonder if they think of me, some visiting each other in dreams, like a secret party to which one was not invited, the solution to throw one of your own and see who comes, how they behave in your house: one, you, I, them, a conversation of hammer blows on wood, a radical lovemaking, rhythmic, without the erotica of flesh to absorb the sound of the strokes. Living on a patch of land that tilts, no flat place to walk but the floor of the house, the bed. A habit of leaning, a feeling of sliding, learning to walk again. But what a gift! this being alive, to teach myself to repeat things as they happen again, the cycles of recurrence, the trap and the pattern, the slow walk over old ground, counting the steps from point of rest to point of restlessness, so that my name disappears into other things, which are subject to the weather, its dangers and its blessings, its not quite accurate memory of what it should be doing where and when, wayward like the inca doves but always there, the fluting call of families in the undergrowth or in quick beating flight above the forest floor, where the sun abandons itself among the leavings of what it encouraged to grow up tall, the great orphanage of fallen children returning as food for others willing to try and grow and be broken as is the story, the energy, endless, relentless, too slow for the mind to grasp.

But at night, with only the clock, it comes as fear. The moment when the last birthday really occurs, and you have reached that age, delayed, but quite certain that you are here, and passed like a row of motels your last alternative, too late at night to choose. So, as is often the case when someone lies awake, you are driving a car on and on along a highway made up of many other roads, and the one beside you may not be your licit mate, but one to whom you wish to tell your story, uninterruptedly, as a kind of ballad whose broken phrases permit no tune, no song, but are themselves a magical release from explanations and doubts, a sketching out of a future life that has happened already in enough detail to make the story true. A story involving walls, nightmares, tigers, infidelities, hunters and hunted, libraries, scraps of paper, poems, Mexican villages, assholes, owls, numbers absent and present, guessed or uncertain, mothers, fathers, telephones, committee meetings and snakes, and the letters you compose but never send, the letters you receive but do not read, the brush with suicide, and the need but failure to kill, the apocalypse of the final letter, Omega, Orpheus, salvage from a fire, the comedy of two thoughts meeting, Odysseus home but to die, a ring of bone, a ring of words, of accidents to come as the car races on. At night with only the clock to listen to you, or by day the wind, trying to set out in detail the drama that is not a pure invention if that were possible, but a way of filling in time with pieces of itself that were memory-lapses, as this morning I couldn't even remember your name, but got it, with effort, when your blind face swam towards me across the pillow. And it was the children who came into the room to complain about dresses you'd chosen for them to wear that helped me remember that you are the one in the car in spite of names I choose as alternatives, faces rigid with inexperience, or with their own experience, which is not open to mine. How can you stand this one who has nothing to say but is full of things to say which amount to treason? The world around us is its own story already told. The rest is like shaking a tree to see what creatures live there by dislodging them, which as a boy I used to do, but as a man I leave them to be imagined. There is no drama in this. And without drama, without the demon playing behind the words, the story can only describe itself and hint at what it might have been, like a cat that eats its litter of kittens, one by one, for no reason you can understand.

"My colleagues leave me cold," said my friend and colleague, and might have meant me too, except that he was talking to me. I sympathize. We are all too busy these days. We have disappeared into our work, which is not our work but our duty to keep busy with, as a way of making the machine that feeds us a burden we can all share, a common act of charity and love. So it is difficult to be personal about anything. Those who lapse drift too far back in the wake before the ring can be thrown, and it is past the time for heroics, when one leaping chance, taking you out of yourself, can make a lover or a friend in a moment, or create forever an obligation neither of you can live up to. "The sign of the eighties is cautious optimism." But it's spring, and my nose takes in the old smells, the exudations of the mother who is not a machine but to whom all machines aspire, even as they violate her while trying to perfect her. I sense a cautious optimism in the night sky, to which I seem to have moved closer, though I've forgotten the names of many stars, memory-points in a heaven which no longer serve me as guides but as patterns of perfection to be gazed at with awe by one who has forgotten his earthly geometry, his ways of walking in his own body, the grace of being in touch with what is his. "When did we last make love?" The body can't answer that question. The mouth can, but doesn't. The act is either an act or it is lost. "Prove to me that we are still in love,"—and that's reasonable, because as life takes so much from us the proofs become harder to act out. The desire is always there, but somehow the acts don't amount to whatever it is the desire asks of us, they are like the stars whose names one does remember, so few in the heavenly scale, attached to nothing but themselves, but they are the only objects you can point to in the sky with confidence, like brief matings on a bed whose scale is time, whose desire and meaning are time. Where is the drama in this? It is too large, amorphous and inert. Better to write an epic about the cut-ants on their hundred yards long journey carrying stolen leaf-parts to some distant hole you can discover with patience. That completes itself, that story works. The nest, the hole, the desire is achieved. Though the whole procession resembles a machine, it takes from the mother and returns to the mother what it takes. What do I take from you that I can return to you? What can I offer you but what I have taken from you, which may have undergone the change of living in my blood but is still, and has always been, yours? Our bodies are bruised not against one another but against emptiness. We desire, I feel, the same thing, but are we the same thing we have desired, so long now, that this earth, this house, these children, are what we have become, are the bodies we have left us to become, finally, ourselves?

This is the final pattern then: not the embodiment, but the completion of these sketches. We do not live in the true southwest, but in this curious trick of history and varied space called Texas, shaped like a child's first effort

at drawing a star. A child's first effort at drawing a star can lead to anything.
Let us see what happens when we try.

Each one of the five points
loses its struggle against
the contradictory pull of its true &
near opposites

A star is born
to frustration. The child has no sense
of the limits which are
perfection of form. The plasma star
crawls in all directions, but is a

star nonetheless with
five limbs: arms, legs, head. Or
call it a star, a desire, a
love of form penciled in light
wanting to become what it
fears most: that
which has nowhere further to go

A man in space
a woman in space, a
code of language: how they mate
& reproduce & speak to one another

in earth's permanent song. And
all roads out of this lead into exile
the graveyard of stars where perfect forms
lie scrapped, their edges rusting

making a kind of beauty
an earth-temple of forms returning
from exile to the mother. Where is the light

born that teaches us
to read our failure into another
better star? A child tries again & again

(but there are limits) to achieve
the imaginary face of some thing both
human & perfect. A poem
set to the music of itself, a star

sketched without any effort at all
accompanied by cries, or the silence which is a cry
resembling his body & soul or the teeth of angels.

The comedy of our times is that people are trying too hard to be funny at the expense of real humor, which is the failure to maintain seriousness. A poem about a star is not like a child's drawing of a star, it self-destructs into its own gravity and self-importance, it turns your attention away from more serious matters, such as: what follows? A man has woken up on his own doorstep, and feels the sun shining in his eyes, burning into the headache he brought home with him and failed to reach his bed with while the moon was setting. It is the season of spring, a little later now, and the man feels the dew on his clothes and skin. He has been somewhere he doesn't remember, with someone he will never see again. Now he is home, and all he has to do is open the door and walk in. But there is a problem. He must invent the story of his absence from home, a story that must sound as if he never left home but was there all the time: a story so truthful that those he tells it to become its witnesses, as Odysseus told everyone he met the most outrageous lies, and was feted for it, and welcomed home by Penelope and his son Telemachus. It should not require a hero to bring this off, or an Irishman. But where does the man begin? Is he confronted by the same wall that kept him prisoner in the first of these sketches: or has something happened since then that has taught him how to improvise and so create, for others, a more convincing self?

So. A man has woken up on the sand, on the shore of his own native country, though he does not know this yet. He feels the sun burning into his eyes, burning into the headache of his long voyage home. His body is still in reach of the sea, its shallows wash over him and retreat, bringing in and washing back the scattered pieces of his text, now soaked and illegible: the words of his journey's story he must now remember and repeat without their help. What should be the happy end is now a further and greater ordeal: not merely to have survived all that happened, but to assemble now as facts the elements of a story that occurred to him as a dream whose details some fool, perhaps himself, wrote down and then destroyed in his despair at finding no meaning in the story or too many meanings for him to tell it as one man's account of himself, before witnesses who were not there, his wife and child. The comedy is that he must be entertaining in this, while his bruised, sandy, sea-washed body, his matted hair and sun-blinded eyes, make him feel it more in terms of moral lessons, destiny, and other serious things. How is he to tell his wife about the pig woman and her island brothel? How is he to believe her when she tells him that, in all this time, she hasn't met a man to better him? What is he to tell his teenage son who sits upstairs in his room, polishing his father's twelve-gauge with a kitchen rag? And how is he to open and enter the front door of what he now recognizes, by signs, as his home, and walk in and begin the thing as if he were a long-awaited god returning, in his potency, from the bitter wars of boardrooms and committees, to embrace them both and drive out all their ghosts? His finger traces a star in the dirt on the porch railing. His head is bent, he's thinking something out.

Meanwhile, somewhere, a sentence is forming. Between logic and the empirical falls the Odyssey, falls the imagination. "When dealing with logic, 'One cannot imagine that' means: one doesn't know what one should imagine here," said Wittgenstein. I can imagine so many things my heart aches with it all. Is that the sentence? Or is that the sentence that says no story, no effort, will do? He comes back to Ithaka to find his car keys where he left them with some loose change on the table in the hallway where the phone is kept. "This dithering leads to nothing but grief," he says, for no reason other than that the thought feels right. Upstairs he hears his wife flushing the toilet, or is it his son.

To have left a wife and son together all night reminds him of other tragedies we have faced, and his mind wanders from the story he is trying to compose to another which he might tell, as a diversion, to deflect the need to explain away from himself and onto the two upstairs, his loved ones. That he does not know his son, that it is not his wife upstairs but his son's mother, makes the story no less difficult to tell. The house looks like his house but it might not be his house, and the loved ones in it are strangers who are loved because they love each other: "his" because they insist on being his, as they need to possess him and be possessed, the obsessive desire for completeness, the three, the family, the triangle: beginning, middle and end. So now he has come to explain why he has been away, and that he has come back to his house perhaps to die and so fulfill some prophecy he never understood.

For I am no longer myself
And my house is not my house.

There are no people in these dreams. There is a man walking upstairs with a story forming in his head, or a man walking up a rocky Texas hillside in spring, with his eyes, while his car speeds west along the rolling four lane blacktop, and he turns to the one next to him and says, "When did we last make love?" and immediately forgets his question as the landscape changes, flattens and becomes more desertlike, and he is on the upstairs landing now looking into rooms, looking into the empty sockets of his own fear, for clues to the story he is unable to tell. I am here and I am there. If you look for me I will return to ask why. We never leave each other in peace. We never return to each other and find peace. Is that the sentence? Or is there one unwritten yet which is too close to truth to make sense. Who is on trial here anyway, and what is the ordeal? Who or what is it that someone must face and give an account of himself to that will release him gradually or suddenly, into a freedom that is the beginning of the same explanation at another level: the terms of which become more and more symbolic to him, more abstract and therefore desperate, as the pattern becomes known to him, and the energy it takes to fail and fail again at telling the story makes it impossible finally for the story to be told? Unless the story itself, in all its terrifying strength and simplicity, is the stumbling block: his sacred truth and also his obstacle. The man pauses. The beds have not been slept in. Who is in the house?

It is the woman who names her son. No man. The seed of ignorance of his ancestors, born into the stillness which is violence, the world in which he has not yet acted out his personal sound: which is already formed and perfect but not yet formed in his mind and by his mind. To have returned to the stillness of an empty house which is his home is like being born, is like the momentary formation of a stone abridging all the years it takes the heart to stop, like this. Violence may be an act. Or it may be the stillness that prevents him from acting when he knows that there is death in the house but he cannot find it, aware, as he has always been, of the hugger-mugger of life's apparent motives, where he is receptive to every small sign but is helpless to arrange the signs in any decent order and follow them to his longed-for but forgotten goal of resolute accomplishment of self. It is woman who names her son, from whose grace he continues to fall as the questions mount up against the affirmation of his birth and name, which are the first and last complete and unquestionable text he will ever have. So now he begins to play with it, to search for the others he has no way of knowing are here, in hiding, and within reach of his voice, his personal sound, if he can find it. Are they important? Or are they masks of importance, held between his face and the sun?

I abandon the bedrooms and walk down the hall to the bathroom. The door is locked from inside. I tap on it but no one answers. I call out, but my voice is muffled against the wood and no one hears me. There are words gathering to meet me beyond the door as I force it with my knee and shoulder, breaking the lock—words of someone else's story gathering to meet mine, as I am now the questioner, the vacuum into which their story falls, not the narrator of his own adventure explaining his absence, but a witness to theirs, preparing himself to listen to what happened in his absence, in the sunlit bathroom smelling of talcum and clean porcelain: the tapestry of someone's experience woven to account for his lost time and theirs, woven and then unraveled repeatedly so that his own story might complete or replace it, if he were to return, if he were not to return, to the sunlit and mountainous island of his birth smelling of olive trees, currants, wine and the ocean wind. But the bathroom's empty. He touches the toothbrushes, and feels that two are wet. He takes three aspirin and drinks them down, washes his face and combs his hair in the spotless mirror where his eyes, suspended between past and future, hang listening between his own and others' lives for any momentary sound that might witness his presence in this story and reveal theirs. The cool spring wind blows in the open window. He looks outside and sees that one of the cars is gone from the garage. My story lacks importance now, he says.

Now he can imagine the mother and her son driving away from him, driving in any direction where he remembers there is a road. But from this point a line goes zinging upward and left in a terrific curve until a nose appears in profile with an eye, dark, primitive, animal, that gazes at the narrator and asks: "Where does this road lead that we haven't been?" Not just a

Texas steer cudding the green wind and green branches of overcast spring, but an eye demanding what, in profile, is the matter with the car, the mother, the son, that they take this road in ignorance of its meaning, of what it might lead them to, toward what husband or father who is not already the son and only the son. The eye and profile in a bathroom mirror, as Picasso might have drawn it, not of a hero but of a man-animal, a story forming in his mind, whose hands are empty: the eye and profile of the driver of the car as seen, peripherally, by his companion who is looking forever ahead and not at him, as the road's future races toward them, and the collision between their going and its coming confuses the story that each has to tell: the place where he must plant his oar in the earth, and she succumb to old age, her beauty gone, and the son go on alone without companions. It is the inertia of those who wait to be moved, who have no will to move, as in the Problem of Three Bodies, where you must try and determine the motion of three bodies moving under no influence but that of their mutual gravitation (moon around earth disturbed by action of sun, earth around sun disturbed by action of Mars) and no general solution can ever be found. In springtime the will escapes, the old stories grow fresh. But who can enact them?

Habits we grow: not to answer but to neutralize the questions.

"I need help."
I offer you my help.
"No. I need help."

Three children in the spring rain, three girls, in the festival of rain, dancing a circle. They imitate nothing they know, their dance is pure feeling. They dance because they feel like it. They feel like the rain. But the eldest, the tall one, needs help with her math question, which is not a feeling like the rain but a problem she can't dance out an answer to: as the boy, driving alone with his mother away from his father, has trouble adding to three, though he knows that three is there, a feeling and not a number, a feeling and a problem he must answer. So when he goes in search of his father, among other men's stories, or tears out his bleeding eyes having learnt who his father was, from other men's stories, he is aware that his own story is something he takes part in but does not create—as this one wanders everywhere but home. The lifeline is the question, is the story. The end is the answer, is neutrality. The fetal question mark lies curled in itself like a seed, and the end is academic: a dot closing off the birth of possible ways to be seen beyond his image in the glass, where every act of his past imagined and real returns to him through his eyes, unwitnessed except by himself, the dancer in his own rain, the father out of season with his children's needs and lives.

And no general solution can ever be found. You are lost among particulars, clinging to the driftwood of what happens, describing the pattern of grain, the texture, the nail holes, with the accuracy of desperation, trying to fight against the entropy that might be your salvation, your way to Ithaka, the island kingdom where you once were king. But the star you followed was drawn by a child, its character was plastic. It has changed since then, it has hardened into a perfect geometric figure whose edges cut, cut away at space, without touching anything live. The bureaucrat returns home, drunk, from cutting at figures all day and his soul's torment all night, to find his family gone, and all his stories of Troy which he had kept to offer them as proof are now his sole possession, as the songs of Orpheus, who was torn apart because of his power to affect others, returned to the wind which was their origin, beyond human interference, the elemental spirit that leads and misleads all tellers of stories, and drives them mad.

What happened to the remaindered songs of Orpheus? Were they sold off cheap or were they pulped? We listen to the wind with the sense that we're hearing words, words of the forgotten singer we think are our own words, and write down as our words, and publish as our words. In the spring and autumn the words are particularly clear. In the heat of summer or in the winter cold the words are intermittent, they refer to no change, either of death or birth, but are words of the dimensionless present, picked up in the street or at the fireside, waiting for time to move. Or do *we* make the change in our lives, as the man in a Texas suburb now leaves his bathroom, walks down the stairs and gets in his car. He sits thinking for a minute or two, because his next decision is whether to go his own way or go the way he imagines the mother went with her son (as this part of the story was not foretold: that he would return to an empty house, with no one to tell his story to, and no one's story to hear) and ought he to have brought the shotgun with him, to assert his rights and prevent something from happening which the mother and her son might later regret (torn, bleeding eyes, suicide with a light cord) or did the boy take the shotgun with him, to assert his right to the mother, and prevent his father's story from having the power to influence all future stories, as it has done? In spring, we decide to return.

The child and her mother lay down to sleep.
Sleep, said the mother, we'll wake up soon
In a world where nothing will hear your song,
Where you will not have to become a woman
And learn to repeat my life, my song.
The child and her mother lay down and slept
In the air too deadly to breathe for long,
And nobody found them until they were gone.

  I wake up and heat a pot of coffee on the electric stove. The bitter taste of waking, sweetened with sugar, whitened with cream. The three girls are already dressed for school and ready to leave. In winter we must wake them up, in the dark and cold of a primitive house, the primitive time of year: light fires, light stoves, as we would keep it that way, "down to basics," the effort now a habit not a plan. But now it is late spring, the longest and most perfect spring in memory here, and there is a story escaping me whose truth I don't feel, of a man in search of something he must answer, some quietus for himself and for others (coffee, life, the implement at hand: the electric stove, not primitive, or subject to fatal use) as events repeat themselves long after they are understood, because the picture was not clear, the picture was unimaginable. The man in his car can't imagine where he is going, if where he is going is where the others have gone, and his effort to imagine breaks the back of whatever story he has to tell, which is not his life story or theirs, but the day's story, the story of this spring, where three girls are dancing in the grass, and there is no future beyond their dancing in the grass, no need to find the mother and her son, no Ithaka, no home. Three girls dancing in the grass, the sun caught in their hair. A hand practicing a waltz on the piano, the rhythm lost in an effort to get the notes right: moment by moment, in sequence, right, so a sentence might form, a story find its direction.

"You should have done your homework."
I need help.

  This other man now, my double, my imaginary neighbor, whose fate is no longer to struggle for home over dark seas, but to go in search of those he left behind, who have left him now, his story lacking importance, and theirs about to begin without him but with him in mind—remember the way you were before you died, the dishes had to be done, the floor swept, and the garbage taken out? Something killed you in an upstairs room, and left a man escaping down the stairs with the secret of what he'd seen. The spring sunlight falls on the place where your body was found. It is not help you need but another story, telling of how you drove west and were never found, not in your identity, not with a son, but alone. There's always this threat, this demon, behind the calm faces of possible alternatives: those who read and watch and are angry because the truth follows a crueler logic than our actions can encompass, making a clown of Oedipus in his worst moment. Turn the page and you might find happiness. You might find a man to care for you, or a woman, for you as you are, in your identity, which now must be established by looking through your personal effects, or relying upon the expert testimony of your friends. Walls only bleed in movies and in dreams. The objective world follows its star the sun, and your part in it is your shadow. *Sabi, sabi*—there's only so much a person can do, like Basho leaving a handful of rice for the child he found abandoned on the road, and moving on, moving north, an old man headed for his own death, the planting of his oar in foreign soil. Leaving his house and going out on foot, when age had come upon him, to meet his end far from home, to keep his shadow moving at all costs until the very end, unencumbered by that child he couldn't take with him for it was only his shadow and himself, walking on, waiting for some place to claim them finally. So this man is free to leave his house and go on alone, or he is free to go and look for those others whose absence makes him feel lonely, guilty and afraid—wishing the car would decide for him, as feet have a way of doing, when the mind is uncertain. What would you do if faced with this decision? Who knows, they might have gone shopping. Who knows. Who knows.

He bores me, this man and his problems. He hasn't star quality. He lacks the vision to return or stay away, he deserves no story, and I can't ever tell what he wants. My neighbor doesn't even know his own name. "We can always choose," I told him one day earlier this spring as he sat in his car looking lost, but he just nodded and stared straight ahead, as if it were the direction and not the motion that was important: the windshield a telescope fixed on a star not yet formed, a vision so distant and vague it had not yet the gravity to draw him on. I watched him sit there throughout the spring and into what is now early summer. I took him food, I talked to him about the necessity of divorce, of forgetting the mother and son who had probably forgotten him. I brought him his mail, and began to pay his bills by forging his name on his own checks, until the forgeries became apparent as I didn't know his name and he wouldn't help me. I tried to explain our double role in this to the police and the newspapers, but all I got was more unwelcome personal attention for one who, being in part his creator now, should have concealed himself and let the man speak for himself, develop some character and decide to act. But he just sits there, the ignition key in his hand, the battery slowly dying in front of him. I talk to him about Orpheus, Odysseus, Oedipus, trying to fill in his past and give him some patterns to move with: but the details of the stories do not fit his memory, which is very literal, as a Texan's must be if he is to get on in the real world. Dealing with him has begun to affect my powers of imagination. I find I must stick to facts at the expense of my own visions, and am being dragged down to his own level of pitiable inertia, while the lovely spring has passed and left me standing at the open window of his car, sweating, resentful, and nervous for my own sanity. I try and tell him that the mother and son who abandoned him will return if he sits here long enough, if only as the report of an accident or a demand for funds sent by a remote lawyer. But he pays no attention. He'll neither stay in his house nor drive away in his car. It is I who must abandon him now and retrieve my self, wherever it has gone, alone or in whatever company.

But I keep seeing a mother driving west, telling me about her child, her son or daughter, lost in time behind or in time ahead. They may be an idea or they may be real, figments of starlight or the stars themselves, so much farther away than the ghosts they make dance in the grass. Fewer and fewer babies slip through into the rubber surgical gloves of waiting doctors. Soon there will be three grandmothers dancing in the grass, full of the signs of spring, of continuing promise of life, and the ghost dance of Wovoka will be universal, though the children in the mountain may not be aware of it, in their separate kingdom in the haunted mountain. They say Telemachus may have married Circe and had children by her: or he married Circe's daughter, killed Circe in an argument and was killed by his wife, her daughter: either of which is a fitting response to his father's life, a lesson in filial devotion or even obsession, the story's gravity drawing him back and away from Penelope towards that other star, mistaken or not, ignorant or not, the need to complete the tapestry his mother never finished. Which may be why this father sits there wondering what to do, staring through the windshield at a vision he cannot recognize or name: the key in his hand, the power at his foot, but the battery gone dead in front of him. He doesn't know those stories and he doesn't remember his own: he has nothing to go on, no star to guide him. Should I leave him alone and call him typical? Or should I leave him alone and call him an unfortunate isolated case, the victim of a great misunderstanding, whose face doesn't even emerge here, who has done nothing to merit our attention at all. He has gone blind, and must hobble his way on a stick to the sacred grove. He has lost his power to sing the great songs that destroy the singer, the impassioned songs that make the animals listen and, eventually, hell itself claim him back. He is a taxi driver in a world of nameless ghosts.

But none of this is good enough. The spring rains have come and gone. The clouds continue to blow in from the Gulf, the low humid clouds of early summer that sweat but never rain: neither mind nor world feels right, they irritate each other, their relationship is intensely uneasy, the one sucking the other's breath, the other fighting to keep it. "When did we last make love?" is the landscape's question, in the trickling sunlight of early June driving west past these hills, knowing the journey is a short one, a relief from the heat of the house, to which the question returns us, answering itself or not, depending on what preoccupations meet us at the door and claim the time we want to set aside for each other—an endless foreplay of necessities amounting to a journey never quite complete, the censored scene in Penelope's bedroom after both had undergone the tests each had invented to make sure. A man and a woman alone now in their house, and those who were part of their story, who died or were left behind, not less than they but no longer the subject now, no longer what the story is about or where it is going, despite memories and dreams which last far longer than the ones whose lives they preserve, which are like waves that push you forward and drag you back until eventually you are washed up exhausted on some beach which proves to be the shore of your own island, the doorstep of your home, with a story of your own to tell and an ear to listen to others, once you have got your strength back and are able to stagger uphill or upstairs, inland to find and create the fate that was promised you, whether the ones you expected to find are there or not, whether or not the ones you find are the same ones you expected, who know or have forgotten your identity and name.

Brother, it's all in the mind, I tell you.
Dance it out in the grass.

Dance, dance until your ghost returns.

But that is not good enough either, not even if memorized and sung repeatedly. There are dimensions and footfalls not accounted for by magic chants invented on the spot. You move, I move, we move, in a parody of the dance our children make. The sentences that must be perfect, the lines that must scan or be meaningless! The precise, beautiful techniques that lead to orgasm, or to disappointment. Such is art, Orpheus—what was your secret? What song could release the spirit of the man who is afraid to drive his car? A lullaby, a psychiatrist's love and attention. *The big horse would not drink water. Injured legs, frozen mane, would not touch the wet of the shore. Flies on his muzzle, the dead river pressing his throat, the agony of snow, wild horse of daybreak. The horse begins to cry, he whinnies towards the mountains. Don't come in! Run to the mountains, the grey valleys where the mare stands waiting. The big horse who wouldn't drink water, the horse beginning to cry.* So the failure to maintain seriousness, seriousness that might lead to acts of suicide or acts of splendor: a prose trot of a Spanish lullaby with bits left out: sketches of a condition where nothing happens but much is imagined, as if future stories cold be composed from these possibilities—or else the story is here, all that it will ever be, already told, as spring passing into summer and now this terrible heat wave demands another sort of words and nerves, a man perhaps unable *not* to move, as all around him is the still and increasing heat of a greater paralysis than his own. They used to pay a storyteller, a singer, for his time, and his inspiration was their need of him. Five hundred years ago

¡Que permanezca la tierra!
¡Que estén en pie los montes!
Así venía hablando Ayocuan Cuetzpaltzin.
En Tlaxcala, en Huexotzinco
Que se repartan
flores de maíz tostado, flores de cacao.
¡Que permanezca la tierra!

was the song of the Aztec poet Ayocuan Cuetzpaltzin, the savant, the white eagle, of Tecamachalco. He sang of the fruitful earth, of toasted maize—popcorn—and cocoa flowers, the plentiful and permanent earth, the standing mountains. The poem is also a prayer against catastrophes remembered and foretold. That the earth not come to an end, the old cycles of the long Aztec year continue as before, the new calendar wheel beginning every fifty-two years with the ceremony of new fire on the Hill of the Star at Culhuacan, no longer a center of power then at the time the poet sang, who was born in mid-century perhaps during the great crop-failures of those years, the five unlucky calendar days stretching to five years of famine and death. The god who is always inventing himself offers no promise of the shape of things. In the blank eyes of the man frozen at the start of the journey he cannot make, these thoughts remain, however vague, an older promise and fear beyond the faces he would search for, bring home, leave home, to recover the meaning of his own microscopic dot on earth: the passion of words open to the sky, beyond contradiction, where he last made love and now tries to imagine the place where it might have happened. It has been a long flirtation, his waiting here. Erotic dreams, words feeling between the legs of words, brief affairs intense this side of childbirth, the freedom to eat the seed before the seed has grown. A mother leading her child into death, inventing and singing a lullaby to quiet its fears. A man waiting to be told what road to take, as a visitor at that grave, his own daughters growing tall in the high Texas sun whose heat eats out the centers of his days. Flowers of cocoa, popcorn flowers—¡*Que se repartan!* Time now to let you drive for a while, face beside me, companion who waits between sleep and restlessness, to take control. The child's amoeba star is drawn but never finished. It has the shape of its maker's imagination, the blind and ageless audacity of this hand to finish what it has begun without end: to construct, in the permanent shadow of a moving cloud, this house where people live.

From *Other Names for the Heart: New and Selected Poems 1964–84* (1985)

Spain

North wind at stalemate with the sun. Acorns
dropping where the wind has touched the oak tree.

You spent too much time living others' lives
casually, as if detached from them. You've

earned the silence you wanted. Now
listen to the replay ... broken glass

underfoot across the red tile floor
of an abandoned police barracks high above the sea.

There is no entry point
no exit wound. But to come here now and think

why such stress still flickers about us like thin rain
the victims dead and gone. You held your sex

like a bouquet of lilies, close to your face.
You gave yourself away at noon like a bride.

Rincón for Paco the Fool

If you grunt you will be understood
to be hungry, but the earth's
lost music is different.

He who walks with the men in the funeral march
& holds the tail of the mule
going downhill
is happy.

From *Other Names for the Heart: New and Selected Poems 1964–84* (1985) 🔥 121

But pointing to your genitals
when a woman passes, is more than hunger
& who can tell you that.
Not the children with stones.

Those of us with voices are
trying, trying
but the nights devour our shadows leaving us
nowhere to meet you.

Sounds. You haven't one word
to catch us with.
But the earth's lost music is different
it is more restless.

I've gone up into the sky my face hangs there
watching for you.

Rincón for the Face in Hotels

Madrid in the rain. Every day
the same fool in the window
mutters "water."

One wind then two
searches the black afternoon light
in the museo del prado.
Yes yes there's been trouble
why did you come.

The black wind & the white wind
two horses pulling a star
it can be fatal

shapes drifting in rain from the mountains
colors drifting in rain from the mountains
mothers fathers names

but on wet days the goats
trot among the umbrellas
along paths near the glass conservatory
goats with eyes like fish.

Northward to Burgos the road
goes up & up breaking through cloud into France
a map of dark colors. The same
story begins to plan
its escape to a better one

some thing with too long a stride
that passed this way crushing people & rocks
all running except one donkey who
won't move.

Grace

for Jim & Cara

I imagined silence was a way of speaking
but it only returns to itself
asking for water. The way they sunned themselves
in each other's shadow, ripening too quickly

in talk too intimate
to carry this far. Are we not made naked
by others' desires? Otherwise why do the mountains
crowd us like a great bed filled with

everything imaginable and alive,
thing and not thing, probing
for openings to our hearts. Her long loose hair

smelling of smoke, drifting like smoke up
from the open firepit. A
whole country in someone's blackened thumbnail.

The Unapproachable

"... the vague, the particular no less vague ..."
—William Carlos Williams

The cure as with a flower is to water the root,
be gentle, precise in whatever you
can afford to give, what it wants.
The crown of lights it resembles are offices
far into the night
                                    numbers giving birth
to new images of the future surrounding you,
and the bridge, the between, stretched
precariously tight from half
to half of what wholeness. Yet

the sun has never watched us,
nor the moon.
Paul Klee lowered the stars
until they hung too huge above our simple roofs,
and a woman turning to a man returns his key
with thanks but regrets. How grave the time would seem
without the jokes we're forced to make of ourselves
suspended like this, as we are,
searching the floor for a lost eye

without which it is hard for me to see
your hurt.
                             And the elevators dream

of going beyond, of lifting themselves high
above the layers of rain, or plummeting down
below the water-thirst of flowers
                             which in your hand
are ghostly smells, colors the night can't give
to anything other than numbers on a screen

as we, to meet ourselves, approach
a mirror placed to make the room seem larger
and are suddenly caught in a smile
both true and false, as the light changes
subtly like a deer running through woods,
but reminding us of blood, and how we tremble now.

Redtails

Always the search for a form
that doesn't resist. That
gesture of both greeting and farewell
perfectly ambiguous, perfectly true

which stops the clock. The sun sets
on the westward cliff, with or without movement of animals

straying through the grass. This is
halfway home, you think
halfway, but why? The ghost of a lyric in a

housefly's wings, the vanished hawks
take only a moment. Is it energy you're wanting but who
can tell us the way, the place?
Outnumbered by suns, by moons

what tower do you climb to fantasize your shadow.

Late Sonnet V

Virtually nothing is whole. I imitate myself in the mirror
combing someone else's hair.
Mornings devoted to traffic begin to seem

like an old path to the village well
whose pure water darkened
for no reason. I try
and the trying tastes bitter. Children

sacrificed at the edge of the well
left their names for others to find like
pebbles and string as necklaces. This

morning you walk out beautifully
to meet what calls you, not by name.

The necklace of stones you wear are my possible lives.

Shallots

She dreamt
her tongue was made of mud.

When she spoke
the little shell-like syllables fell apart
as her tongue dissolved, no one

understood her. In the rain
her eyes stood as two pools
where someone's fingers had poked holes
and left them for the tide to fill.

Now
her children wonder where their mother went.
They finger their eyelids tentatively and
curl their tongues in the soft earth of speech

and breathe quickly, like children treading water.

Polonaise

We drink the rain.
We open in the sun
but between these there are weeks of darkness
or hours when the light dries us

to a tense whisper. My blood
left me and curled up under a stone
in the canyon bottom. Your walk
as you approach this shadow is innocent

but movement is never innocent, it
attracts things, the prickly pear
this effigy with pins stuck in its heart

which stands for patience. We

don't go back there anymore. I wonder how they felt
waiting in line to be shot while the wind just stood there.

Scavenging

Winter vines running like flames
across dry hillside. We speak
of fires we must light, of sleep, like the ghost
of a dead woman who visits us only to go

backing out a door
which is all doors into darkness
words can't open. The remaining grapes are soft
and taste too sweet

like the eyes of asiatic orphans
left to contemplate too long, but we
pick and fill a sack with the best we can find

and return at night at the same steep angle
awake and thoughtful. I've lived
unnecessary lives fingering what comes to me late.

Visitors

for Christopher Middleton

Where there were houses there is grass.
What we missed were the shadows
the sun crackling off
painted metal. A few thin trees.

We say we miss that, but the
photographs had it wrong, the latest
evidence shows a family no one remembers
posed in front of a lake

before a low sun
cutting into their eyes.
The shadow of a tree just touches
the man's left shoulder. The woman

leans down to speak
to one of the two girls. The
dogs that run everywhere looking for water
left prints on the muddy valley floor

which have dried. Something went wrong
with the mathematics, with the camera.
There is nowhere to settle here.
Nothing to settle on.

I scrape a bent, rusty nail
on a stone, to see if the metal will shine.
They walk their ponies back up through the grass
that covers the hill. They do not look back.

Snow Country

for Avanthi

Kawabata talked about
the "roaring at the center"
deep in the mountains when snow
has covered them. This

is the sound of distances made
heavy, and bare of all details
between your blood and nothing.

Early in the day when things wake
listening, to be sure it is
the same world. And if
not, what power is there to make it
reappear (wind
is not a substance or
your breath on the mirror) the

picture you imagined,
come down to earth
like the angel in Tolstoy's story
to help you tie your shoes. A
child walks out the door you locked last night
and you hear yourself asking the time
in an empty house. It is

so important. Something to fill that
foot or so of space you're afraid
to leave. Why is it possible
to imitate almost anything but
oneself, the distance that listens
and has no answer? Because you dream at night
you are naïve

and nameless. Your helpless throat
drinks dust among sparrows.
Pretty soon, you say, pretty soon
I will look at you out of eyes
that have learned, in exile, how to fetch

things back, from that space between
a world I had composed

and this one which breaks me. Is it
that serious? Your
shadow like a pietà, limp in your arms
but carved hard in stone. There is
no voice at the center. But as
Ponge imagined it, "then the nocturnal
outcry reverberates," and

between your blood and nothing, in that space
where you were last seen alive
the mirror reforms, a fish swims at its edge
and amazes you. How many words does it take
to redeem one? The issue
is not love. That word is broken.
To wake up in the mountains, cold

with first snowfall, it could be memory
asking for food, a
child now adult gazing past herself into
the mirror of the wind, not lost
but patient. Your vision of being
at one with things is hard, not easy.
Your sense of being separate follows, it

resembles despair but can
still speak. When you leave
abruptly the door swings
like a body that can't decide
which way is out
and must guess its direction. Like Yoko's eyes
in the snow story, the girl whose body fell

dead through the flaming house, beyond words
or love. Only her leg
moved slightly. That is the feeling of silence
the cry at the center (not voice)
no one hears. You melt with the snow,
just the slightest pressure.
He lifts you up and takes you to the window

naked, to look at the white world
to look at the mountains.
This is the end, the departure, your
self from self, your substance from the mirror.
Distance takes your hand, the train comes in
leaving a sound of breaking glass.
The mountains, only the mountains.

Other Names for the Heart

This feebleness, this trembling
at the edge of self. Robert

Schumann suffered fits
of shivering, apprehensions of death.

Fear of high places. Fear of all
metal instruments including keys.

The note A sounding always in his ears
later became voices. His

piano returned to the silence of wood.
The air that gave him music

reverted to air. Wind, and rain on the window.

What do you listen for? The earth
is wounded. Earth cannot make you whole.

Spirits of the old
earth return, yes, they
linger and confuse you. Yet we are bodies

and sometimes, when the light is good
we move as music, we compose ourselves
in patterns of exact time

and dance as blood to blood, the piano
silent, the melody only in ourselves.

But it takes the courage of gods
and we are human. It requires

what our eyes refuse to see
to see ourselves, as Schumann
dragged from the icy river, the Rhine
in February, quite insane

saw or
felt himself that night
breaking the surface, the cold flow
of time his hands had touched so masterfully.

Other names for the heart, all
obsessional, like the heart itself

rise like bubbles of air
the breath we keep or lose. Some boatmen

found him and pulled him to shore.
What they rescued was a question answered.

Neutrons

When the wind blows
you often get this feeling
somewhere there is a city
that does not feel it

the city that is
not the citizens
who are part of the wind
who appear and disappear
like theorems on a blackboard

It might be
that up in the Generalife
among the cool, perfectly silent cedars
philosophers and mathematicians
meditating, talking among themselves
knew of this wind

The precise desert voice
returns to us now
as we stand high above the world
thinking of the tribes that will live
and those that will die

the numbers we call passion.

Cante Hondo

At eighty-two her great artery
broke in the old woman. She
fell and they laid her out
on the white reddening bed.

Now after the funeral
the mattress and sheets are piled
at the back of the house.
Tomorrow

he will take them into the field
and light a match.
He will burn the blood of his mother.
No one else can do this.

The Conquest

I lean into the crowd and ask
who is it what happened

there are streaks of sky across a puddle
where sailing ships move
hinting at new discoveries

the beginning of a green coastline
fringed thinly with blood

and someone says
it was my mother it was my mother

but what happened
whose

voice is that singing the ave maria
repeatedly like a hungry animal

I watch and learn something
of the inconsistency of laughter
faced with sudden rain

Inktonmi, a Prayer

The companions of Red Horn return to their homes.
I mistake my flesh for meat
and eat it. In those days
the summer was kept in a bag
tied to the lodge-pole. Precious things.

Trickster why do you bleed
from the anus when you could have helped me split these logs.
Winter is almost on us, on our backs.
I am the last to know myself.
It is down to bone. My body

feels its ancestors stirring in anger, in
bewilderment. My children find in me
a mother with dried breasts. They
cry for my attention but
between a man and a woman there is so little to say

that has not been said
in better times. We must reform ourselves
against the contempt of things that knew our

touch once. I do not know
if I have the tools to do it.

Paracentric

"As one grows older one becomes
less clever and more personal …"
from the notebook.

                 There is this solidity of things

which vanishes. Or you see
only the bones
not the lovely body walking with its books
on the grass, under the high sun.

I wonder what my ancestors would make of me now
crowded into this space I have called
my self for too long

                 this sunlight

I feel I don't share
and am jealous of. The old

crazy connections fade
before some need to survive, to feel
the gravity of the long invisible line I have been
walking

                 which I perceive now

to have had its
fatal colors, misdirections, smells
I attached to those I loved

                 and thought my own.

To accept this change
is an exorcism
but not an answer.
Something primitive in you cannot plead
but must accept, like Oedipus
                    exile and grove

to the turning of some moment when his hands
cease to be strangers who had done those things
and the bodies return, living, naked
with words of this world
                    foreshadowing another

and another
daughter who will live and bear your name
until her change comes
and the light returns
in ways you could not have invented.

From *Figure of Eight: New Poems and Selected Translations* (1987)

Premonition

She kicks off her jeweled sandals.
The rain will wash her feet.
The long hair of the rain
will hide her eyes. Any moment
the way is lost and must be looked for
without footsteps, the gaze
always the gaze, breaking
through heavy cloud. Wild animals
living the night through their eyes
as we live by fire, whisper
this is not the way. Turn east, turn west
plod north or glide to the south
it is all one where the spirit stands
barefooted in the rain
waiting. She gathers the young trees
and eats them leaf by leaf
drinking the rain. Blood collects
in the footprints she leaves behind.
On Broadway the lights flash out her name
a hundred years from now, the
wind that turns the rain-wheel
rises and dies, circling her feet.
She moves as a flute breathes
through all the stops and ghosts of air.
The lights flare in our bone-cells.
It rains as it never rained.

Figure of Eight

"En la bendita soledad, tu sombra"
—Antonio Machado, *Del Camino*

"That girl standing there"
—W. B. Yeats

I

Frost a little like Yeats
a great poet no one wants to be
caught dead sounding like

and Pound might have got it wrong
but Lowell's excursions into history
were fruitless, mirrors just

to magnify the self
and diminish the anguish of time

What Pound suffered at last with the Jews
was incarceration and the threat of death
the wages of love, to survive this

but eventually the stories get told
yours, mine, in whispers or through
that silence which is terrifying

because it is "its own nothingness"
the gap in the journey that annihilates
the entire road. So far one goes

has gone, must come again
to where the pathway and the feet
are identical, and you are not

the figure lost or I the shadow left.

II

That afternoon
the rain came
riding the back of the wind
we watched, naked behind the screen
and couldn't make love, the wind and rain
did it for us, and you sang
a love song from your village
it moved in the wet air and rush
of water through leaves and grass
the trees shook their ankle bells
and flung their hands
"an unbroken continuity
of existence in itself"
to borrow words from Jean-Paul
who was as remote from that moment
as you are gone now
beyond the Manhattan skyline
city, city, the great divide
the "empty world of laughter" as you put it
to walk out in the lamplight
as the snow drifts down
a hundred years ago
an hour from now
"for the most beautiful girl in the world
can offer only what she has"
that circle of light in the dust
which Lakshman drew around Sita
to protect her from her story
the imperative of her own fate
the passion of rain falling
bent-headed into open hands

but she went back under the earth
and Rama grew tired of life
and crept to the river's edge
and vanished as a fish slips through its ring.

      III
While I was making coffee
this morning in October
a coral snake climbed up a dead ivy vine
to the window sill, its tongue alert
for early autumn insects

pretty the quick black eyes
I checked for holes in the screen
the fissures in my own skin
and watched it swing slowly from vine to vine
in a pattern remembered from dreams

repeating the dance figure
anchored at head or tail
of your feet on the boards of the stage
the lock and pivot somewhere in
the lifeline of the body

at points that varied, as a poet will
his rhythms, or a dancer's breath
then loosing its grip to fall
flat to the ground, its whole length
never the head first

a moment to recover
then the slow crawl, this cobra relative
through the skelter of ants at the wall's foot
like Pound in the tent at Pisa
to learn it all again

from memory to climb the sunlight
genius of beginnings with no ends, life
forever ahead of the sentence one reads
or creates, as
your body in repose, your body

wanting our eyes wants more
breaking and saving the figure, the double
circle of time returning on itself
both snake and dancer
patterning as did Yeats, or Frost the native

or as Lowell wanted, something too close
two bodies at bed in the heart
the earth-smell stronger than either
the beauty of nature in no way
comparable to that of art, which is its own end

(to paraphrase) and yours
pretty one, the kiss
between us this distance now
and "What is this separation?" you ask
the sunlight and October air

this nothing and all .... Insect words
flit at the tip of my tongue, the dead
vine my lifeline even as I crawl
hungry into winter. Love
I eat my words, am filled with emptiness.

IV

They brought him hemlock and he
drank it like a snake
his dancer's mind accepted
the body was old and should go

and form was everything
form, the pattern, the artistry as it
touched on things and gave them shape
shape to live by, shape to die

the thread through which the spirit moves
that breaks and remains the same
in the anguish of knowing
nothing lives up to itself

or can ever return

An old man falls into silence
having said everything
and finally "I was wrong, I was
mistaken"

but nothing can change that now
the enormous tragedy of the dream
is the form the body is left with
the pattern it leaves
                    is silence

and every voice that ever spoke
the sadness of your eyes in repose
the dark light of laughter there

after love and rain.

     V
Do cries fall
in the category of silence
            the thought itself is enough
hidden away in a blood-cell
or a stone cell underground

how the body survives
what it knows is not the favorable air
of successful laughter, irony
of ironies, *iron maiden*

Osip Mandelstam
whose muse turned to hunger
in deep winter
       the cry the silence
edging into daylight like a spider
when the light fades

the one circled by nothing
the eye ringed by her admirers
the bride, her bachelors even
soledad

to live life to the hilt is such a
strange expression and must relate to
battle or murder, how
       else to draw the bull
onto your sword
who love that kind of dance
necesidad

which way do we go, what is the *tao*
who haven't phoned or will not phone
so long or write a simple note
or send it

if we are nothing and must create ourselves
as the wind creates deserts, trees
and gardens, excuse enough
       the tuft of inky hair

soft where my fingers enter, make
the rain-dance

is memory
bitten tongues and words lost
in the wet silk of open mouths
commingling, dry by morning

how to be clear without confusing
issues which are forever confused
by definition, so
                wild the silence, its cries
of ecstasy, its unbound hair
the poet searching his garbage heap
sweating and freezing

"that beauty may be
in small, dry things"
an antidote to all this dampness
like a laundry line
                the Indian cotton print
torn beyond wear
washed and kept as a keepsake
vanidad

What gathers here
has no way out.
I open my hand and release
the invisible thing with wings.
I release you, your shadow is heavy.
The *mudras* change, your hands make
"a woman becoming two birds."
You are out there now somewhere.

VI

My mother goes out one door
My father the other

the stage is empty, the theater
is full of invisible eyes
nothing moves

tungsten bears the silence
the light, well past the melting point
of human nerves

tension, at the point where lovers
break and separate
and the children continue to wait

watching that last place
where the two cast their last shadow
the invisible door that opened once and

closed .... The way you look for
is not the way. We are free to choose
what is visible, visibly ours

the thing in hand, the captive.
When the sun falls in just such a way
on that yellow stucco wall

something that flies away and hides itself
and later calls long distance
teases you with yourself. Your

being, your not being there
in the closest to touch I can come.

VII
"Ill fate and abundant wine."
—Ezra Pound

The lives of fragments. This pathetic duty
to pick things up and put them back
where they belong. To tidy
the edges of life
so the center is clear, the circle where
you alone stand witness
to an orderliness which is forever
breaking and scattering in its own helplessness
what you love and protect with your life
or things simply gathered, how
to tell them apart, your
self from each one.
                    Dumb things without mouths
that shine in their quiet pleading to be kept
a little longer.
                    I sent the box by freight
five working days to the tenth floor
New York address. The pink towel, the small
tape recorder, a *Norton Anthology*
some school notes and ball-point pens, the old
leather sandals ... miscellaneous things
from the past now coming to crowd you.
I kept the little copper bell
that fell off the anklet, I keep
too much to myself, I take, misplace
things where they are not. They dance
a silent pattern on the carpet in the shadowy house
singing under their breath
so only the blood can hear it. As
my father would whisper her name

while he went about his carpentry
or stood at the sink rinsing things
over and over until we took them from him.

Summer too long where is fall the keen
Canadian wind
the clear streambeds of eyes, the
lassitude of honey.
                       Means and ends
"The honey of peace in old poems"
the clear viscosity clouded by the cold
of living fragments.
                     Why should the agèd
men, old men
should be
beautiful manners
                a life for a life
for a time, picked apart like Penelope's threads
so the figure can return whole
in the mirror of the silent telephone
the unforgettable voice
at some number listed somewhere in the sky
of its lights at night
                The box is sent
filled with oddments … a photograph
someone took of you in bed
who loved you but never touched you
as these words attempt to keep that touch
the wind knows and is expert at,
no human.

VIII
Not enough to speak the language of one's time
there is no such thing. Or to love

the lovers of one's days and nights
who are ghosts of others, who mourn
for you and for themselves.
                    The name of this one I speak
over and over in the air she left
behind her. Name me, name me too.

The *peripeteia,* the journey never over nor
long enough. On a rock at a point where the path
turns, she is sitting, her face averted
waiting, waiting for something …
mas Ella no faltará a la cita, the
loss of others to others, or
to the expert wind. The merest change of light.

Matsya, the fish, the first
to come, the first
to return, among
the incarnations if
the circle holds.
                    To know
the dancer from the dance, her hands
that make the shape of Krishna's flute
or fingering more intimate things in the ever
questioning never ending
city night, the bee
enters the flower, the flower
opens, and closes.
                    Name me, name me then.

Brahmins not eating fish or flesh
for they are the forms of creatures that God
has taken in time, though man
eats woman, woman man

and the tree spreads its shadow over all
the north wind brings cold rain
the cigarettes are empty
                        Name me then
as another. Its own nothingness
returns as a figure of speech, a
paper or bamboo bird hung from the curtain rod
in the window facing east, a tender
photo of a *geisha* with a paper fan
too young to know much
                        someone's child
about to become
another's girl. Name her for me now.

No more elegies, *no más.*
So far one goes the long way home and on.
The light has hands and turns itself
so slowly from frown to smile
the day latening towards the coast
in sunlight on a clear road with the tape-deck playing
the light back to you
                    the evening *raga* sung
in the raw voice of the sea
the three descending notes repeating
                    naming you again
asking you to return. And you are gone.

En la bendita soledad, tu sombra.
In the blessed solitude, your shadow also.

Interstice

Deep as it appears to have gone
the way lies deeper

depth of rivers, depth of eyes
depth of hidden intentions

the hazy wind, the *amargo*
sea wind flutters in the tv aerials
above the village

some things move slightly
and others soar, it is all one body
a scarab, a mountain swift

the goats are coming down the mountain
leaping and jumping over the rocks
the thorny bushes

somewhere not in sight
a car is burning by the side of a road

nothing is there to watch it but these words

Patterns Leaves Make

The adams and eves are in the gallery.
In separate rooms the light changes
differently, my
remorse, a clock
running down.

In sugar maple weather
hands taste sweeter.
I dream I believe. A dusky skin
glows between buildings, moves
just out of reach. Your breath

is the silence it takes to speak
what is listened for
but might change. As a painting
turns from you and re-enters
the landscape it came from

or that face
already moving away
to ask its question somewhere else.

Of the light in the park.
Of one particular tree.
A perfect stranger.

Proof of How it Should Look

We asked for proof
of how it should look.
Our hands were full of shadows.

Something in the grass made us turn
to listen, and at sunset we stood
wanting proof there was
something there. The wind blew your hair

back, like strips of dry cedar,
sun-fragrant, and the grass

was listening for us to move.

I had a time in mind and you
another time; this looking west at the air
hurrying to reach us, the
shadow climbing our bodies

as if to see beyond us, farther than
why our hands weren't touching,
that we stood so still.

It is nearly October.
We have been here thirteen years.
Something moved in the grass
and didn't move us to move,

to turn, to listen. We are
eyeless like the trees now and
as sensitive to change, the rain

darkens our skin, the wind dries us.
How could we help but ask
for proof of what it might become, this
tension that cries in us to be.

Spain and Kafka

I

How exactly the paler shadows of the
black iron railings angle away
from the source of light, the white
house-fronts deepening as the
sun climbs. Their lines

straight or bent depend upon the surface
they cross. You watch, no two are alike.
But in memory they lose this, they
revert to the perfect symmetry of remembered forms
and faces, the
geometry necessary for patterns to survive
and be remembered. I think I could
draw that house in detail, remembering it,
but not your face, so wide across
the cheekbones and eyes, the way your
hair falls. And the outline of those mountains
so clear as I look at it now, would be
impossible. No
concept or abstraction
would capture that shape of time, its flow-lines
too much like memory itself to be remembered.

II

Formal demands, clear cries for help
from the senses—
dark falls in the room
where one cricket sings
invisible but everywhere
turning the black air into
white sound. He dreams of Felice,
not herself but the details she
reminds him of, his
memory's icon, worshipped like the nerves
he's cursed with. To know
everything, to be in touch without ever
touching, to stay beyond reach and
feel, hair by hair
her head forming in his hands, her
face her eyes but

incalculably distant, as if she has
died already and he
loves her for this, the details
too real even to be true. But her life
plain and solid, evades him
who feels the wind in his bones
the mole's terror in a human kiss.
"Someone must watch, it is said.
Someone must be there."

And Language is Everything

This philosopher I knew, his
baby sat in its highchair
and was attracted to the flame of the match
he'd struck to light his pipe.
He gave it the match to hold and it screamed.
"I love that child," he said.
"I want it to learn the difference between
appearance and reality, brilliance and fire."

We left the house and watched the cool stars forming
familiar patterns, as our eyes adjusted.
I thought he was right, and that the baby should kill him.

Assia

If I am to stay where you put me
give this note to the one who was expecting me

a white ribbon tied in her hair
unraveling now. In the doorway of that

shop that is about to close
how to tell the difference, but for the eyes
concealing the knowledge of a lost property
as a light that is fading. Who

of her own dark generation having escaped
to live this long, who, of her wandering kind
solo now, the stage hers, weeps silently.

The woman who waits becomes
less and less visible. When night falls
she is the whole of darkness waiting to go.

Climbing

I noticed in the mountains this time, seven years later
a configuration of myself and you
as memories of each other, the one
ahead, the other behind, climbing
in the same place. It didn't seem right to be here,
to have repeated this
time and place so strong and the same figures
retarded by this: the
man and the three children, and the fourth
who was not born then: reliving for ourselves, our
selves the fact of our repeating this, as if
too deliberately, as proof we were not wrong
about something we knew by heart, only
ourselves? The old trails, sharp with stones

peppered with goat-droppings
didn't know what we were asking. And there was
a reluctance to use the camera, a
desire to get beyond range of what was
obvious, while yet repeating
the obvious, as we have always done, and the children too
by habit. But this place was too important.
It had fed us too long with a vision of what we might
really become, not for the
asking, but for the
taking. These mountains beyond range of our home
above valleys of tragic olives, suffering for rain,
too strong to be held close: the fine line
between wanting and having, memory and repetition.
I make too much of this. But without this question
it is all a painting of solid primary colors
arranged in patterns a child could grasp
as a child climbs, easily. Or as our life has been
the effort of unraveling fear, without breaking it,
so as to be attentive to rain as it falls
and feel at our roots the air the rain won't open.

From *Child Eating Snow* (1994)

Baby Upside Down in a Light Snowfall

The ones we know and recognize
through the flame, they smile and are gone
before we can name them   As memory is
what otherwise we would forget
what cries for forgiveness.
The mouths   the tiny mouths of snow that burn us.
The white nails of our mothers playing us wildly angrily.

Child Eating Snow

for my niece Sylvia

In the wilderness she
imagined she grew up in
there was this photograph
of a child eating snow.
Handfuls of years
back behind memory now
and not her face at all
the eyes different
like a bird's eyes
eaten out by the wind.

II
In the winter sun that year
her father was all bone. Slowly
he was turning white
like her shadow on the snow.
In her dreams she never saw the sun
but sometimes a vivid suffusing light

like a torch shone through water
reminding her
of the first cry
of her birth.

III

On the tenth of March
a door opened somewhere along the horizon.
Her father left her. His dark eyes
return at night, beyond the stars
behind the snowflake.
The bird cries again
Cry I can't imitate
No eyes it has

IV

The blue static of lights along the freeway
grows colder, turns warmer
turns to flame. *Snow*
is how mirrors looked
before I was born the old woman remembers.
The sun squats in the grass
like a dam-bear. It is brown like her father's eyes.
Silent, as a mouth stopped with snow
her memory of this picture.

V

She sits in her mother's shadow.
She is eating the snow from his face.
Winter whispered her name, summer will
sing it now. The
single bird's cry
is a forest of music of leaves.

But it is still winter she said.
It is still February in my hands.

                VI
The day is at breakfast.
Things, things to do.
Will the clouds leave the windowpane?
She's skating on last year's ice.
Wings hover above her, soft
hunter's wings. *Falcon, soul*
exiled among ravens, Father, your shadow.
It is summer.
The sky is mother blue
in the winter she imagines
she will live in forever.

                VII
The child is eating snow.
Her hunger is her thirst
her thirst her hunger. Her
father dies, her mother is alive.
Between seasons she draws breath
like a creature in hiding, to survive
what might watch her too long
too intently for love. So
she whispers her own name
Bird, how old am I
How old
is the rain in the summer grass
beyond mercy   beyond memory
Bring it to me. Bring it now.

Exuberance (Paul Klee)

As I danced along the tightrope
I failed to see
the figure of a woman
in dark mourning blue
lurking in the lower
right-hand corner, watching
her back pressed
against a patch of red

the same red that surrounds
my face my beating hands
not the sky blue that encloses
the upside-down man falling
the exclamation mark at upper center

there are greens, there are other colors
at lower left a tiny dog
or deer, a straw star
high up, and a hand
above the woman's head
or is it a crown of fire
and the black scorch marks in opposite corners

teetering on my rope
I danced with all my hands
it was 1939
I failed to see the hidden
woman shawled in dark blue mourning
in one corner
I failed to see

dead center
the booted man in brown with huge shoulders
beginning to scream at me.

Separation in the Evening (Paul Klee, 1922)

Two arrows point
from earth to evening
evening to earth.

There is the ceremony where the two meet
and never meet, like our tongues
touching, or our tongues
speaking. One

descends from dark violet twilight.
The other rises from sunlight
in its earthiest desert colors.
Together they are everything
that begins invisibly and ends
invisibly. In the few inches between

the meeting of the arrows
I touch you now.
I try to touch you now.
It is where the space is neutral, neither
sky nor earth, and your
lips are open. It is the wind

we both imagined was our bodies.
It is the evening.

Paris, 1957

A Citroen Deux Chevaux
parked against the curb
on a rainswept boulevard
and passing this side of it, her
heel lifted, a hurrying woman
whose shadow falls towards me

is how the dead might see us
at play in a photograph
no colors in their world but
light and shadow, and very little light

(or lovers the old hotel
whose name they've forgotten
the street, the exact address lost
off the edge of memory)

anonymous and lovely
the car in the rain, the shadows
the woman hurrying along the wet street
are all the mother we have
who watches us, late as it is.

Poem Depending on Dashes

But here with winter about to begin
a cold whisper in the leaves
and the woods full of ghostly deer

hidden between cracks of sunlight, where
looking I see only my old self
in a still place, a posture of waiting
the gun, the loving fingers of
those old vanished habits we shared
one autumn, or was it ten—
before something or someone called you
but—and the words that come now
Love is to me that you
are the knife which I turn
within myself—are Kafka's
by accident I recall, more than chance
which is a touch different if only
less violent—here
in this house farthest from your life
but which I imagine I love
as I can imagine we loved
despite all that happened, death, death
and your death—
the leaves ask no questions, or the grass
lacking the thousand human mouths
that are born to cry and devour
what we are, what we were—But
I am what remains of the eyes we shared
the noises, winds, voices, smells
as if it were a single animal
haunting itself—the shed trees, the
stamped lights of houses along the road
back, always back to this—the leaves—
the sentence never finished

Namelessness

By now after all these years
I don't know who the "you" is any more
when the word writes itself instead of a name
or an honest detail. I had forbidden myself
this vagueness, this evasiveness
which is like the shadow that follows this pen
across the page. I had said
honor her memory, or hers, or hers
or speak of the subtle dark one I am with
who asks, what am I to you, am I
nothing? I have fallen into this habit
of remembering what comes easy to the heart.
You have no name. There is no smell in you
of skin or hair. Your body's word is gone.

Old Legends

Where the wind goes it breathes
sometimes such damaging testimony
that I am at a loss to know
who sent you here. You were one
to whom I said I love you
not enough, or was it too often
for both of us. I sleep badly nights
imagining how poorly we both lived
what was given to us, a kind of beauty
that need not have depended on others

who said they loved us. We did, we do
ourselves such fatal injury. Now
I confuse you with what I remember of you.
We are such shadows. Yours is more alive.

Ethnic Poem II

A baby hung in the wind
from an apple tree. The hills beyond
seemed high and endless, there were
patches of snow on the fields
or limestone showing through the grass.
Though the picture told me no date
I had come here before, whether by foot
or by horse and in whose company
I couldn't remember. And this time
the baby seemed more personal, a
thing I had been sent here to account for
to imagine its name, its father's eyes
and mother's hands. They had said
you will come to this mountainous land
and find there what you came to find
far from your own life and touch it
and give it your name. Is it
a girl or a boy I asked the lingering wind
for nothing else moved. Then let her
remember I came. Let her hear at least
my footsteps on the loose stones
as I walk away and do not look back.

Night Bus South

I might have imagined the voices singing.
To our left, a pressure of hillside
lights of Monterrey and the higher stars
paler, just as close. So when the song
came to me, riffling through your hair
like a vision of night insects without wings
I thought the voices were only part of your dream
a bend in the road south, day waiting for us
ahead, in a new country. Then I wondered
if the night wind—or was it just one
of many possible sounds—had let me remember
a younger journey, alone, away from one
whose hands are now cold: a blood song of dead stars
I touch in your wrist, its pulse alive, still warm.

Beyond

Night of south winds! night of the large few stars!
Walt Whitman's voice crying out
to Pablo Neruda in Isla Negra, Chile
a hundred years beyond. But tonight

I press my ear against the soft bark
of a dying live-oak tree. Its roots are remote,
silent: they confess no pain, they
have no voices. What to save

what to let go. White, edgy leaves
scattered like manna across the grass.
I put on the tree's age, I wait for sunrise

about which it knew so much and so little.
I gaze beyond at the far, light-flecked hills.
The homes there are worth millions.

A Window in London

Who was that you saw walk past
turn and stare at you and go on walking
up the street to the left of your eye
then returns and stares right up at you
while you hide behind the curtain edge
not afraid but unwilling to be found
your eye gone inward now, the square
of autumn leaves the beginning of cold winds
imagining a figure seen through glass
looking not for you but for her now
and how do you say she is gone
before the horns of winter and the cold
catch her, the flick of a lighter at a
cigarette the room gone much too quiet
and the stranger prowling across your eye
how will you get rid of him
what will you do with yourself.

Vigil

I was walking alone uphill
with my car on my back
when the car became a backpack
and somewhere I lost it. Child

I had warned her long ago
the minute you spread your wings you risk
disturbing some god. Look here
at this refuse of old books
the kind no one would read
the kind you find in old hotels
in colonial towns, shelved behind glass
while waiting for someone to come
who said she'd meet you here
but is late. And the light grows old.

An Event About to Happen

It was taken in the late afternoon
by a steadier hand than mine.
There is a smell of late snow
and cold patches of thawed grass
her shoes are wet with it.
The tree she leans against is an oak.
Distance is caught behind her
like a long rope thrown over a wooden post
the afternoon still against the blue sea waves
some marlin fishermen running for open water.
My hand brushes this mirror, touches
a blue dress hung out to dry
at the season's cold edge
waiting for someone to claim it
or disown it. I imagine wind
riffling the branches of her hair
as the oak tree waits for its leaves.
Her name leaves no shadow. The sea

the fishermen are far away now.
There is no cry. There is no negative.

Bettelheim

I had finished washing up
wiped my hands and turned the light down low
when the trees west of the house appeared to move
slowly as if following the sun down
the farthest woods that let them filter through
trailing their hands to be touched
one by one, and I heard
human names. And a phrase *the terrible silence*
of children came to me from a book
the work of an old man who died
touched white with grace and suffering
if that is ever a grace. And I wondered
how many of those silent survivors ever found
themselves. For the dead they couldn't mourn
there can only be remembrance and yet
the children of those who disappeared
their eyes like empty spaces the trees left
in the cold abstraction of grief why can't we
speak to them? I mistook
the ghosts of children for the shapes of trees
trees for the shadows of children
tree-ghost, child-ghost, selves lost in selves.
And I am haunted by a need to forgive
and be forgiven that cries beyond my voice
to the silence of children whose lost names
are the dead who hide beneath these words.

In Late June

But for the tapping of a hammer on wood
the light is going nowhere, the green
of the early sun fired to near white
in the elm leaves. A few old
dry ones flitter down into the too-long grass.
Birds waiting before the heat to come
talk quietly about personal matters
secrets I try to distill from words
that have no song or color and can't fly.
It is sometime late in life. I am here
at this moment. I am here and every place
and moment I have ever been is here.
The wind rises, the disorder of quiet air
reaches for me, and I breathe again.

Conversation

I have this habit of talking to you
when you're not there. Your absence gives me time
to explain why it is I love silence
as much as you need voices. When
we are together the silence tilts towards you
and takes your name and eyes. It
leaves me and becomes your need to remember
something important, something perhaps very small
that being forgotten has the power to kill
us both. I knock three times on wood
for the shadow who lives in our bones
grants three wishes. The first is memory.

The second is that the secret you remember
is worth your life. The third one has no face.

Heat Wave

It is these nights when
the work of being alive goes on
long after the sun has gone
and you yourself are the shriek of the cicada
when after the light has gone
the heat of the solid dark
cries within your cells and will not
scratch or wash off. It is
waiting for the hours of the pale clock
to fall exhausted into another dream
like the one lying awake
imagining Paris and Helen hot
in the archaic night of far clearer stars
that lit their way from breath
to breath at the cold end of desire.
It is the way you lie there
waiting to be picked and eaten whole.

Summer Morning

You must get up as early as the light
a fine tremor that is more like water
a tolerance of the air, early morning.
Your eyes have waited all night
to open. Your eyes have waited all night

to come to life. You see the world
you saw fifty years ago but had
no words for. Having the words
now makes the light hold still a moment
and the moment resembles your life
as a dry leaf hangs and spins on a thread
of web off an elm twig. A mile away
the sound of a truck engine revving
burls through the river valley
like the sudden memory of forgetting
a name whose life depended on your own.
And memory and light seem identical
the calm witness come to detect again
a look in your eyes, a child's question
asking what day it is, an aging man
or a woman afraid of growing old
while the light speaks to her. You see
what the trees could always have told you
if the wind had left them the words
if the light had given them mouths.

From *Solo With Grazing Deer* (2001)

Lamp

While I was dreaming inside my flame
the wind bit at the edges of my teeth
and I thought I could see in the dark—
it was your word against mine.

Though they had broken shattered pieced together
Dresden and Hiroshima
Coventry London Guernica
the shadows you left wouldn't move.

So in Robert Capa's photograph
of a street in Bilbao in 1936
eight women and men and a young girl
look up at the sky at where German bombers

are coming. So it might have been
a little before dawn when a boy not quite one
woke up in a white crib in Yokohama
and saw shadows cross the ceiling of his room

—the world had soft bones
and old and brittle bones
and from time to time the light falls
exactly where the body runs to hide.

Sabi

I feel my rust beginning.
It is inside me and between my fingers
a slow cold itching, like distant rain.

Or brown eating at the edge of a leaf
which is the light withdrawing
the mirror withheld
the air's child that hides.

The sun tests the future with a tentative hand.
I know the gender of water, the cold
beginning of memory under the long evening light
that comes to no fulfillment but itself.
The light that keeps returning has no language.
I am content to remember how you breathed.

Rune

Under the wind there is a place where you can hide.
Think of it as a silent event. An evening comes,
and you are ready to tell a story you have never
heard, tell it in such a way that whatever secrets
you had gather around you now to listen. They have
no name but yours, and they are still listening.

Landscape

In autumn the silences grow loud.
The sounds become echoes.
I have been gone a long time, they
changed my number, the branch
I hung from has been cut.
In the room the shadow dolls
play across bare walls, there are

fresh spiders. The music I heard came
from outdoors, celebrations of air, wind
rain, at the ear's edges, listening.
Why won't you come in? A traffic
of handcars running along rails over
loose coals. An engine starting stops
abruptly. The silence is like a brush across
dry canvas, like slow fingers playing
through pubic hair. A white cat sits
like a harp on the window sill. It is
cold in the mountains, after a summer
training my eyes to see
what they once remembered. I note
the place where my chair stood
a square of pale light on the grey
carpet. What would you like to do?
The soup kitchen, the popular sushi bar
usually fill by noon. The river
below is the color and chill
of fish, my fingers go numb
winding and unwinding this wet string.
You used to play an elegant piano.
Now in the place where the piano was
a crowd of echoes cries circling
desperately to find your hands. We are
out of touch. A sudden dash of rain
wets the glass and moves on. Tires
in the street exhale through wet teeth.
You were impatient with me. Three
seasons out of four the room chose colors
we both liked, heights of canyons brushed
with a first snow, brown shadowed by deep
green in the conifers just before dawn.
The patch of shadow where night

lay still in your armpit, a smell
like riverweed a moment out of water.
The almost white room is
emptying now. It is a book with blank pages
or a book whose familiar pages have faded
to this. There is no eloquence like
whiteness and silence. There are no
words where words end. The
room is empty now and white with shadows.
Black forest against white mountains
far away. A lone crow flying.

ᚱ

I am drawn to *bèi*, the Chinese cowrie radical
in its simplified form, how it resembles
a hidden man stepping out cautiously
in the shadow of his hood, off to the right
as all characters move to the right
if they move at all. Cowrie shells
were money in ancient China. The figure occurs
in keeping with things of value, commerce, trade.
But I think of him walking the streets alone
night and day, with no thought but to hide himself
like Camus' stranger or Eliot's compound ghost
the masked spirit of some truth whose voice
and silence keep the broken sun from rising
too soon for us, who choose his company.

Stump

The burnt-out house we are always
afraid of. One open
upstairs room made over to the
voices of stars, a song
beyond itself returning to our ears.

In the beginning the shadows of our hands
played with us, the shapes
of light before our bodies could crawl.
I remember the old stump
where the tree was. Darker clothes
that hid my mother's face. The
soft laundry folded by the years.

When we were young
the answers were what we touched.
The grain of words was something less than paper
more than the wind. The rain
brings me to you. The rain that
precedes fire, that soaks the hard dirt road.

We all rise too early
or we sleep too late. The
golden grain we ran through down to the valley
is the texture of a painting. Where the
roof was, where the stars
kill time. I have

trouble now imagining where I belonged
and in what season, whose house this is.
My grandchild's eyes are bright water drops

in the night sky. She is new to us.
We hold to what we have. We hold hold.

Railroad Tracks, House for Sale and Clouds

She left us while the light was bad.
A sudden movement on the hill, pepper
shaken from heavy clouds.

Someone kept asking, who?
But in a voice I didn't understand
like rain in a dry field, remotest echo.

The sweep of the long field slightly uphill
framed by two eucalyptus in the midground.
SEVENDE ESTACASA. Silence of afternoon.

And the tracks long long ago abandoned.
Grey deliberate rails from left to right
and back again, the eye the only pilgrim.

From left to right and back again
across the high, brown, dry sun-tipped grass.
Like her mind, like that dead tree.

Or the other one fallen on the roof
too frail to break the tiles, or the hill line
beyond, where we saw her move.

And the clouds darkening now,
the fire at their edges softer, gone.
Snow in the Andes. Hail on the lower fields.

How memory brings us to a place
then hides like that, leaving not even a name.
I call and hear nothing but holes.

Happiness

No one goes to the park in winter.
Quiet hands, eyes, there is little to speak of.
Absence is a color not a sound.

Unless when the sound dies it becomes
the color white, as in a Chinese story
by Lu Hsun from which the opening line

of this poem comes. There a thin man
a good teacher who lost his job, a misanthrope
who loved only children, died

spitting blood, like a red sound on the snow
white of Chinese death. So this park
where I think the two of us walked once

I've forgotten if we ever came here but
we lived close by, whatever the season was
it returns to me now as a place filled with voices

I thought were ours. I open this book
and the pages turn to leaf and winterbrown grass.
Over it all broods the distant waking sun.

Wild Eyes

I have set plaster to catch a foot.
Who is the runner who passes every day
                    leaving nothing behind him.

As the rains begin
autumn is still a ghost
or an unborn child waiting to name its mother.

Headaches and the rain!
In mourning for his dog the poet wrote
                    dog a thousand times.

At three in the morning the sun is too close.
How can I organize the events
that led me here.

                    Where

is the money. What time did the train leave
bearing away my sins
the memory of my father ending with me.

Frictions

A man running on a background of wind
among graves. Where is the suit
on the empty hanger. How long
can I play.

The picture of a heart done in blue crayon

on white paper. Somewhere
they exchanged eyes.

A man running in an unlucky direction
calling out to someone. The light is against him.

The light is in his eyes
as the trees turn the leaves burn.

As the leaves fall *fric fric*
on the dry pavement. How far can he run
calling calling against the hurt light
his hands reversed
his head and feet

reversed. The coat hanger and the man
are both naked. Something

fell on the roof. Something
falls on the roof
where the house stood.

This is a painting about a change of season
a change of heart affecting the mind of light.

So little time to notice little things.

Sunlight Through Blinds, Four O'clock, Facing West

Whoever comes stepping through the frame
make it worthwhile for us now.
Beyond the trees there is a river

and beyond that a dark headland
knifed by the prow of a long canoe
forever still in its movement.
And my eyes fail, and give back
whatever it was they saw
whatever it was they understood they saw
for it is blank now. I go to live
in some future of memory among
the howls of the skins of dead animals
who spread their soft-eyed bones
over mountains and plains and through towns
where the light picks us up and walks us home.

Answers

What is the time of day
listening in a stone
warmed in an old woman's hand
on a concrete bench
in a square in an old town

a name older than mine
though grass drifts in the air
at the same instant I hear
the wind blow her skirt from black to shadow
like weather changing

when we return from war
when they returned from wars
the garden was always there waiting
though the postcards have turned brown
a dog's jaw buried to help

corn or alfalfa grow
a superhighway crosses the bridge
that connects time as it joins
both shores that long ago were one
was it her dog her garden

her son who didn't return
is she Dolores or Maria
or Kristen Helen Angelique
waiting for the sun to marry the wind
like weather turning

a name older than the town
an older name than any town
the square the fountain named for who
first put it there
no clock heard anywhere

to what lover she gave birth
who drank her wine and left her dry
the wind to blow it all away
as footsteps up the rocky path
the stone drops from my hand.

Departures

They hung
stations from her eyelids
with real trains—
Anna, or
whoever takes her place.

Across the wind-darkened harbor water
white sails. Mud and rain
tracked in on children's feet.
Where, where have you been?

The lonesome train of her heavy century
long gone. Explosions still to come.
For me, a silence
in my ears, a winter
haiku—

Shimogyō ya
yuki tsumu ue no
yoru no ame

> *In the lower town*
> *across the heaped-up snow*
> *whisper of night rain*

One is so frail.
Two are hardly better.
They were jackhammering the street outside
a day before the news came.

I like to think the snow
will give her back her shadow.
Milk across darkening grass, the cold.
Daphne gone to tree,
doe-ears flicking.

Time Out

Out there, rain telling the trees
to repeat their leaves

Father, you are the shadow
I stepped from

You I haven't talked to for years
bear with me

Out there, the rain
saying nothing but rain

saying this.

Solo With Grazing Deer

Mother's son, father's son.
Late spring, the rain hangs on
like lost sleep.

A smell of fresh soap
when the wind drops. In the field below
a horse neighs. The wet cedars

bend to earth, looking for their roots.
Waxwings tilt and soften
the grey air between branches.

Memories still to come
like waves that haven't yet happened
gazing out across the wall of sea

to where the sea ends. The deer
gone. Myself I've been saying goodbye to
all my life. Beads of rain

like a series of clear names
run together. One, then a
thousand. Then the whole sea boiling.

From *Asterisks* (2007)

*

3.

Two branches
Two birds
    one eating
    one watching

if one were to fly off
the other would have no purpose

More to
where you are
than
here I am.

*

5.

The lifesnake uncoils
into that hole
where water
is driest   On a billboard

a woman is swimming
away, toward sunset
   and life returns
      where you were

rain silences by touch
the apple of thought.

*

9.

This mark refers you to
another place
        fire, her star
an unpronounceable name
whose wherebeing
        kept old light

She had a way with her
What lovers saw
        or missed
in her eyes
was an ancient event
a murdered light
        gone black

Texture of an empty chair

vacated air.

*

11.

Dreams: radical doors
forever open, closed

Wake at night to the crying of a spotted fawn
taken by something—

unknown yet familiar
city of strangers
all on first-name terms
          whose meanings are forbidden

Here there has been a death
or a vanishment—
self, cold-case detective
in search of his shadow

          too late, as often
among the clueless footprints
leading here or there

choose whichever.

*

12.

We come home in the sense
there is that,
waiting or gone.

          A deep
vowel draws us. Otherwise
what lurks in pastures
or lingers in dark city streets

is air that touches
nothing.

          An old sandal
its mate lost

is home. The air
in an emptied pen.

Not examples, images.

Memory of a loving hand
stroking
what night
makes afraid.

*

17.

    They scattered the fires
and rode on.
       A few bones
catch the wind and drift off as ash.

What talk costs…

In the future are settlements.
Now
dusty soldiers go elsewhere
and breed new freedoms.

     Have a good day.

We in turn
sleep less
and make it count.

*

19.

The knife-cut knuckle
almost hides its scar,
        my singular addiction
to old wounds.

In the village street
a drunk fell
and crawled away
up steepness into darkness.

Dry summer, dry year.

Then that night, a sprinkle
"Rain," spat José,
"I call that bird-piss."

The pictures faded now.

Old olive sacks
the memories
ripped and tossed aside.

*

21.

Tu Fu: "How will poems
bring honor?"

I cut at this—
So that we talk about—

beauty of
fine language.

The soldiers of dust
want to come home now.
Blood mixed with dust

is metaphor.

As dying is like
nothing.
        Help me ask

a question that has no answer.
A poem nothing can read

but itself.

*

24.

Village, hills, blue sea

You look for something
that isn't there,
so you invent the thing
you're looking for—

Wheat, olives, vines, figs
the plains for progress
the hills for mere survival

Same crop at different altitudes,
different harvest months
but the same prayers—

Earth, heart,
opens so very slowly

rain, wind, sun
and the swallows come and gone
each one nameless.

*

27.

One by one they go
        the old languages
                the little tongues

Birdwings heard at daybreak
they enter and leave
the back way—

There there
old ones
        old songs
                old bones of songs.

*

33.

If it is the nature of women
to scream, and men to shout
the rest, by right, is silence.

Snow drifting over our
forgiven names
whiting that human darkness.

I love the evening sunlight
north of the house. Her voice
from the kitchen calling me, come help.

Heaven is dry of blood. Air
fills the veins of the saved
whispering, mercy, mercy on us.

Such little breaths
from which the rain comes.

*

36.

A hand raised
in greeting, or
to ward off the sun.

That, I say
is my brother. Walks

with the slow gait of a horse
or wind through the tall fieldgrass

across forty-seven years

pencilmarks
by the kitchen door

lengths of children
his years so much less.

*

44.

Here, there, memory fails
made up by threads of fiction.
Something must fill the holes

the spaces, the silence
so the fabric holds.

You are now my creation
as I am in part yours.
Stupidity, happiness, pain

we are one landscape,
where the light was once at home
but moved, has moved on—

wind above the mind, running, walking
the quick bodiless presence.

You, said the old one, and you,
join hands now. Be careful.

*

45.

Subject to object: sun wind rain
joined in ways language has
no hands for.

Words precede the unborn life—
hopes, fears, a name.

The homeless poem
grazes alone in some neighbor's field.
Lightyears are its substance.

It leaves no evidence
it was ever alive.

No soft prints in the snow.
No feather falls from the sky.

I am open
says the door.

*

49.

Not to
say something, but
to say
toward something, I think

says it.

In an hour the sun will rise.
There are no clouds.

Watch with me.

Part Two 🔥 Translations

Introduction to Ferenc Juhász

Ferenc Juhász was born in 1928, in the village of Bia in western Hungary. His family were peasants. He grew up as part of this peasant community of village and farm, and moved to Budapest in 1945. There he studied art and began writing poetry. His earliest collections, published in 1949 and 1950, won him much prestige and the important Kossuth Prize. To many at this time, Juhász seemed to embody the spirit of Petőfi, the great nineteenth-century poet of Hungary: the same sweeping, epic talent, an awareness of the aspirations of the Hungarian people. But as events changed in Hungary and in Juhász's personal life, the poems became more intense, more self-involved: a dialogue between the poet and the wilderness he filled with pre-historic creatures, proliferating flowers, mythical birds, and a sense of dis-connection, bewilderment, strain. "In the years 1957 58 I could not work. Many questions troubled me, besides I was ill for a long time. I thought, I have to begin everything again ... even the language has to be made new."

Juhász has written more than any Hungarian poet of his time. His poetry is uneven, and his energy is colossal. His poetry comes from the grassroots of Hungary: the peasant traditions of folktale and ballad, super-stitions, the cycle of life and death. He has a child's eye for nature; a mare with her newborn foal:

> And the foal slept at her side,
> a heap of feathers ripped from a bed.
> Straw never spread as soft as this.
> Milk or snow never slept like a foal.

And in "Comet-Watchers" he describes how the entire village rushes out to watch the phenomenon in the sky:

> Over the hill, the star-freaked sky
> blazed brighter than burning hay—
> a stallion with wings and a diamond mane,
> a mane of fire, a streaming tail of blood.

There is an affinity between Juhász and Marc Chagall, a "natural wonder." But a poet's world is not so hermetic as a painter's, and as Juhász begins more and more to look around him, his poetry becomes darker. On a visit to a church in Batak, where 4,000 Bulgarians were slaughtered by the Turks nearly a hundred years ago, he is reminded of man's struggle against oppression, and asks:

> What happened here? What does this crying emblem
> mean, here in the heart of the church this once-
> soul and marrow-gifted crown?
> It mourns the madness of power, greed, pride—and the dignity
> of defiance, passion of man and woman,
> for you, you earth, the fiery unquenchable core in us
>   Liberty!

The poem, with its refrain "bone, vertebra, skull," is a cry against violence and tyranny, and is Juhász's own cry of defiance, his attempt to state his role as a poet. The poem is written at white heat, condemning the "human pig-killing," the "blood-guzzling" that could happen again if people let it and the exalted sanctuary of the mind, the church, become a "stone coffin."

> Bones, vertebrae, skulls … enough.
> Can my senses still live with this sight,
> this heaped imagery of horror?
> Is there one cell left in my body
> which hasn't suffered the death these bones did?
>
> Is there a cell in my brain
> that isn't part of this grandeur now?
> Have you an ounce of shame left,
> poet? Shame for yourself
> as you stand here, in a white shirt, a summer suit,
> on the stones of this church in August '52?

This poem, "A Church in Bulgaria," was a declaration and turning point for Juhász. Not overtly a political poet, involved in his own imaginary world, his poems nevertheless begin to reflect his own mood and the mood of the country, as he feels it, more and more. Following Bartók and Zoltán Kodály, he goes back to the ballads and folklore of Hungary, to a deeper vision of Hungary, away from the apparent futility of the present, the emptiness he writes of in "November Elegy"—

My mind hunts in circles, sober, ruthless and cold.
The dull tapping of autumn rain numbs the soul...

where he talks about his "stunted dreams" of "revolutions not fought," and is reminded of his isolation, his sleeplessness—

... And even if
sleep comes, will tomorrow waken anything?

In this poem, and in "The Seasons," a personal lament written during his wife's illness, there is despair. But the fertility, the noticing things, the involvement with man, animal and flower, is still there. Juhász's fertility often leads to chaos. Many of his poems are wild, organic growths that get out of hand. No detail escapes his attention. What the gardener plants he becomes part of, gets carried away with. But from this nexus have come some remarkable poems.

The greatest of these, perhaps, is "The Boy Changed into a Stag Clamors at the Gate of Secrets." The poem is a long allegory whose form and theme have roots in Hungarian folklore, although it is an entirely original creation. It is a poem of two voices. The mother, alone in her old age, calls out to her son to return, tries to lure him back with pleas and motherly promises. But the son has been turned into a stag: he can't return now; if he did, he would destroy her and desecrate his father's grave. Their voices arc back and forth across the poem, calling, answering each other. The mother's world is the home, the stag's world is the forest: the forest of the past and the technological "stone forest" of the future. He stands "on the crest of all time," at the "gate of secrets," from which there's no turning back except in death, where he and his mother will be joined:

Then you can lay me out in my childhood home,
with your age-veined hands you can wash my body,
close my eyelids, swollen glands, with kisses.
        And when the flesh falls off me,
and the stench it was sweetness to flowers,

I'll be a fetus drinking your blood,
I'll be your little boy again...

"The Stag" has affinities with Bartók, particularly the *Cantata Profana*. The structure and rhythms of the poem derive to some extent from the *regös-lays*, the shaman-songs of ancient Hungary, where there is a magical creature called the Sun Stag who resembles the magic lamb in the ballad "Fair Maid Julia:"

It carried the sun and moon between its horns,
It carried the sparkling star on its brow.
On its two horns were Ay! two fine gold bracelets,
Ay! at its sides were two fine burning candles,
As many as its hairs, so many the stars upon it ...

who in turn resembles the stag in Juhász's poem:

Each branch of my horns
is a coil of gold rings
each twig of each branch
is a candlestick cluster
each fang-sharp tip
is a fine funeral candle ...

which, as the poem develops, becomes:

each prong of my antlers a twin-legged pylon
each branch of my antlers a high-tension wire ...

"The Stag" is the finest example of Juhász's use of folk tradition and ballads to create an original allegory that is both personal and universal. It is a total creation that carries all its levels of meaning along with it: the past to which one can never return, but to which one must return in order to find meaning in the present and strength to go beyond. It is where Juhász cuts himself adrift from the powers and certainties he relied on in the past. Like the poem "Rainbow-Colored Whale," addressed to the grave of his father, it is a summation and farewell:

Life here is peaceful
without you.
Flower then, flower into
the death-wish of the lily.

Juhász is a poet at odds with his time. His weapons are not irony, allusion or insinuation, but energy, imagination, and a passionate "Hungarian-ness" that he gets from his peasant background. His poetry shows very little literary influence, none of the fashions or styles of the time: he is a native product, touched by surrealism perhaps, whose real roots are in the ballads and folksongs of Hungary. His own vision of Hungary, with which he identifies himself, isolates him from the "huge merry-go-round" of the neon world he sees developing around him where, in the city on a rainy night, he sees the "neon monsters," the beasts of the past return:

A bestiary
of red, blue, green and yellow faces ...

—a world where man walks alone, where it is "not permitted" to cry out or complain:

Where am I going?
What song am I singing?

Juhász is disillusioned with man's ability to accept substitutes, the artificial—to accept them until reality comes, unrecognized, and destroys him. He has tried to create his own mythology, to express an elemental vision, a totality however chaotic, to set against the world of statistics, paper forms and evasions. His enormous body of poetry is uneven. But he's written some of the finest poems of his time. Speaking out for himself and, one feels, for Hungary, he ends this last poem, "Thursday, Day of Superstition":

Hell-bent on life, like a sponge, I head for home
in the red, green and blue rain: in the age of socialism.

This selection of Juhász's poems was chosen by Flora Papastavrou and myself. I do not know Hungarian, and these translations could not have been done without Mrs. Papastavrou's insight, imagination and enthusiasm. She did the roughs, and unlocked many of the poems for me by her interpretations and suggestions; so it was a joint effort. I would like to thank István Siklós, who read the manuscript, made suggestions, and provided me with notes. And also the National Translation Center, Austin, Texas, whose grant helped me to go on with the work.

D. W.

Ferenc Juhász
Silver

The traveler stands in the freezing cold
surrounded by drowsy old men.
His moustache is ice, his eyelashes
inhuman half-moons of silver.
He stands watching the horses,
the snow dusting under their hooves
like a cloud of millions of comets
misting the milky star-roads.
His ears are silver, his hair is silver.
The horses twitch their manes and tails.
Silver the velvet nostrils, the steaming flanks.

Gold

The woman touches her bun
of thinning hair. She laughs,
and drops a spoon and a hunk of bread
in their reaching, grubby hands.
Like roses divining water
the circle of thin red necks
leans over the steaming plates;
red noses bloom in the savory mist.

The stars of their eyes shine
like ten worlds lost in their own light.
In the soup, slowly circling
swim golden onion rings.

Birth of the Foal

As May was opening the rosebuds,
elder and lilac beginning to bloom,
it was time for the mare to foal.
She'd rest herself, or hobble lazily

after the boy who sang as he led her
to pasture, wading through the meadowflowers.
They wandered back at dusk, bone-tired,
the moon perched on a blue shoulder of sky.

Then the mare lay down,
sweating and trembling, on her straw in the stable.
The drowsy, heavy-bellied cows
surrounded her, waiting, watching, snuffing.

Later, when even the hay slept
and the shaft of the Plough pointed south,
the foal was born. Hours the mare
spent licking the foal with its glue-blind eyes.

And the foal slept at her side,
a heap of feathers ripped from a bed.
Straw never spread as soft as this.
Milk or snow never slept like a foal.

Dawn bounced up in a bright red hat,
waved at the world and skipped away.
Up staggered the foal,
its hooves were jelly-knots of foam.

Then day sniffed with its blue nose
through the open stable window, and found them—

the foal nuzzling its mother,
velvet fumbling for her milk.

Then all the trees were talking at once,
chickens scrabbled in the yard,
like golden flowers
envy withered the last stars.

Then There Are Fish

Forever confusing smoke with weeds,
clouds and sky with water.

Born with no lungs, just a blister
floating in a cage of splinters,
listless fins and hyperthyroid eyes.

Even the smallest fry
chase their hunger as boldly as carp—
mouths, nostrils, eyes
burst on a rising scream like a shoal of bubbles.

A world of nothing but water!

Houses and trees
float up like giant bubbles.

Comet-Watchers

One blind-calm summer night
someone tapped at the window of our house—

"Come out! Come out!
There's a miracle! There, in the sky!"

We jumped out of bed. What is it?
Some secret message from the stars?
I grabbed my mother's hand, it was warm,
I felt her heart beat in my palm.

Barefooted, in shirts and underpants
the whole village gathered out there in the cold;
scared old women, sleep-white faces
frozen in the white light of another world.

The poor came crowding into the street.
Women crossed their arms over their breasts.
Their knees shook as they gaped at the sky—
a fairy tale, a holy prophecy!

Over the hill, the star-freaked sky
blazed brighter than burning hay—
a stallion with wings and a diamond mane,
a mane of fire, a streaming tail of blood.

I gripped my mother's hand like roots.
I remember the warmth of her body still,
and father pointing up at the horse
blazing away in the fires of its own sweat.

Proudly it flew away over the roofs.
We stood, still as gravestones in its fierce light.
The sky was much darker when it had gone.
O fate of comets, will o' the wisp, our hope!

Mary

Like a little cow swollen with calf
she moons around the field, cow-eyed and staring.
The moon's silver belly hangs low in the sky,
the moon beginning to ebb, and the seas
ebbing with the moon.
She remembers the horde of children
locked in their room, shouting, their faces
pushed between the window-bars,
heads poking out to spy on the world,
red eyelids, petals of blood-red rose.
She loiters slowly away
like a little cow swollen with calf,
her rump swaying as she ambles along.
Above her the stars shine hard and cold.
Her heartbeats are too loud …
she doesn't understand … she stops,
looks down at her belly, and feels
the little feet kicking like a heart.

The Tower of Rezi

I sit here in the Rezi tower
under a massing of swallows—
through my field glasses I follow
their soaring, darting flight.

Below me the yellow harvest land,
poplars and mown fields;

the old forests shedding their leaves,
mist melting distance.

My eyes are glassy stalks,
they catch a swallow as it dips.
It is held in the glasses' lens,
trapped, in a fairy-tale glass tower.

The wonder of this magic spell—
modern wizardry!
It flies so near it's as if
its wings would flit through my pupils.

Inside me now: it dips and dives,
curves, wheels, flutters, drops
(through my body) so lightly,
drunker and drunker with the wind.

I can feel the flutter of lungs,
the ounce of heart's motor—
rib cage, feather, tail—
lawgivers of the flight's arc.

And I'm flying—it's me, not the bird!
the wonders this lens can do!
The self swirling and dipping
forgets it is only watching.

I'm a spiraling, tiny
swallow now. O you swallows!
I'm hurried aloft and held in the arms
of endless space.

My heart has become a bird,
put on feathers, grown wings—

I share
the soaring infinity of the bird.

Most wonderful, wonderful flight!
Joy, pain, sweetness, tears.
The circling heart feels no boundaries,
each curve brings it nearer to heaven.

And I know, what traps it too
is the huge eye of the lens
(for it wants to escape)—already
its beak makes signals of distress.

Then suddenly, in a careless moment
it breaks from the path of the lens—
swallow, where are you? Heart?
Torn clean away with the rest of the swallow-flock.

Through the field glasses I search
blue nothingness.
Nothing but the infinite there.
What happened? Am I left with no heart?

November Elegy

My mind hunts in circles, sober, ruthless and cold.
The dull tapping of autumn rain numbs the soul.
Rain drips from the ivy leaves
in heavy, sticky threads: earth, sky, the roof-eaves
sweat with fever. Soon there'll be nothing alive!
I can't sleep, my mind has lost its wings.
My brain is a live coal, the bedclothes are flames

eating my bones. Ships' horns
cry from the Danube. The light from the street is sick,
it throws ghostly leaves on the wall, and tricks
the still, painted horses in my friend's
picture—whinnying, they dance from their frame.
I put my arm around you, your touch soothes me.
Under my hand your breathing is poetry,
pulse, rhythm, ebb, flow, the heart's knocking.
But sleep won't come, the rhythm's lame, and shies away—
the clear voice of sleep can't sing
my stunted dreams: of revolutions not fought,
memories, fevers, desires that swirl in the heart's
bottomless slush, churned by the killer hooves of contradictions.
My soul steams and smells like vegetation
after a sulfurous summer night of storms.
I get up, stand at the window: hollow, echoing sounds
from the town below, a baby's cry, an animal wailing.
Nightsmoke lies in the trees, reminding
me I am alone, how alone.
That sound I heard was the last tram flashing home
over the bridge, writing its sign in the rain.
And now, like someone slowly crossing the room,
a scythe taps on the wall … hallucinations!
I must lie down and rest. Sleep, so the nerves and brain
can heal. And the heart, the idiot heart.
My eyes burn, I can't sleep. And even if
   sleep comes, will tomorrow waken anything?

The Boy Changed into a Stag Clamors at the Gate of Secrets

The mother called to her own son,
cried from far away,
the mother called to her own son,
cried from far away,
went to the front of the house: from there she cried,
unwound her heavy knot of hair
dusk wove to a shimmering bride's veil
that flowed down to her ankles
a flag, tasseled, black, for the wind
the firedamp dusk that smelled of blood.
She knotted her fingers to tendrils of stars,
the moon-froth covered her face,
and like this she cried to her dear son
as once she'd cried to her child—
stood in front of the house and spoke to the wind
spoke to the songbirds
to the love-cries of the wild geese
shouted across to the wind-fingered reeds
to the luminous sprawled potato-flower
to the stocky, cluster-balled bulls
to the sumac tree, shade of the well,
she called to the jumping fish
to the welding rings of water—
    Hush! you birds and branches
hush, because I'm calling
    be still, fishes and flowers
be still, I want to speak
    be quiet, breath of the soil
    fin-quiver, leafy parasols
be still, deep humming of sap

rumors that seep from the atoms' depths
    bronze-chaste virgins, wool-breasted flock
be quiet, because I'm calling,
I'm crying out to my own son!

      The mother called to her own son,
      the scream rose upward, writhing
      spiraling in the vortex of the universe—
      its blade glittered in the light
      like the scales of a spinning fish,
      like metal in roads, niter in caves.
      The mother called to her own son:
come back, my dear son, come back
I am calling you, I, your own mother!
I am calling you, I, your riverbed
    I am calling you, your fountainhead
come back, my son, come back
    I call you, your memory's teat
come back, my son, come back
    I call you, your ragged tent
come back, my son, come back
    I call you, your guttering lamp.

Come back my son, I'm always knocking against things,
I have bruise-stains under my eyes, on the skin of my brow,
my calves, my thighs—
objects charge and butt me like angry rams,
the garden stake, chairs, the fence, gore me terribly,
doors thump me like Saturday drunkards,
the light's broken, the switch gives me shocks,
blood crawls in my skin of veins as through the beak of a stone-bruised bird,
    the scissors swim off like metal crabs,
matchsticks hop like sparrows' legs, the bucket handle hits back—
come back, my dear son, come back

I can no longer run like the young mother doe,
    my legs are ripe with bindweed,
    knotty, purplish roots grow in my thighs,
my toes swell with calcium-mounds,
    my fingers stiffen, with flesh tough as shell,
like snail's horn, scaly, like old shale-rock,
    my branches are sickly, dry and ready to snap—
come back, my son, come back
    for I'm spellbound,
    haggard, and full of visions—
    they flicker from my decaying glands
    as the winter morning cock-crow
pings off the frozen shirts hung on a fence—
I call you, your own mother
come back, my son, come back—
give meaning to all these things,
control them again: tame the knife,
    make the stubborn comb show itself,
for I'm just two green gritty eyes,
bubbles of light: like a dragonfly,
    which as you know, my child
    carries between its nape and jaw
two crystal apples that fill its whole skull,
I am two huge eyes without a face,
and their vision is not of this world.
Come back, my son, come back—
    breathe life into things again.

      The boy listened,
      he tossed his head,
      with nostrils like pails he
      sniffed, his dewlap quivering—
      his veined ears pricked at the sound
      of that crying voice, his body tensed

as if sensing the hunter's footstep
or a whiff of smoke in the forest
when the smoke-blue forest
mourns its own burning, whimpering.
He swung his head that way
hearing the familiar voice cry,
suddenly stiffened with fear—
on his rump he noticed the fur,
discovered the split hooves,
stared at his cudweed shanks,
at his furry buck-apples
hidden there, where the lily shines.
He galloped across to a pool,
his chest ploughed through ferns,
body a muck of foam,
gouts of lather smacking the ground;
his four black hooves
stamp life from the flowers,
a tiny lizard is squashed, its
crushed neck-bib and tail grow cold.
He stoops over the pool,
stares into the moonlit water—
a beech tree with the moon in its hair
shudders—the pool reflects a stag!
Then he sees that the thick fur
covers his body all over—
fur covers his knees and thighs,
his tassel-lipped penis sheath,
and antlers grow from his head
where the bone-branches had budded,
his face is furred to the chin,
the cut of his nostrils slanting in.
He whacks his antlers against a tree,
his neck a rope of veins,

paws the ground, his nerves strain
choking to bellow a cry—
but it's only the voice of a stag
his mother hears echoing back—
he'd weep the tears of a son,
and blows till the watery monster is gone,
blows, and in his breath's whirlpool
in the liquid midnight sparkle
little fishes with petal fins
scatter, their eyes like diamond-bubbles.
When the water's feathers settle again
it is a stag that stands in the moon-foam.

Now the boy shouted back
    bellowing, stretching his neck
the boy shouted back
    a stag's voice wildering through the fog—
mother, mother
I can't go back
mother, my mother
don't call me back
my nurse, my nurture
mother, mother
marvelous foaming spring
roof I grew up under
breasts with swollen buds
tent sheltering me from the frost
mother, my mother
don't ask me to come
mother, my mother
my one silky flower
my bird of gold
mother, mother
don't call me back!

If I were to go back
my antlers would spear you,
my horns: tip to tip
I'd toss your old body—
if I were to go back
I'd tumble you on the ground
with these hooves I'd squash
your little breasts
my horns would stab you and stab
you, I'd bite you—
I'd trample your loins
if I went back
mother, mother
I'd rip you soul from body
bluebottles would flock to it—
the stars would gape
in shame at your soft lily-cleft,
though this gave me once
such lovely, tender warmth
in its luster of oils,
warmth such as the breathing
cattle gave Jesus.
Mother, mother
you mustn't call me—
you'd turn to stone
you'd die, if you saw
your son coming.
Each branch of my horns
is a coil of gold rings
each twig of each branch
is a candlestick-cluster
each fang-sharp tip
is a fine funeral candle
each lace frond of horn

is a gold altar-cloth.
Believe me, you'd die
if you saw my sprawling
antlers filling the sky—
as on All Souls' Eve
the graveyard is lit
by candles, leaf by leaf,
my head is a petrified tree.
Mother, mother
if I found you
I'd scorch you to
a blackened stump,
I'd burn you to a lump
of greasy clay,
I'd roast you to chunks
of charred black meat.
Mother, mother
don't call to me—
if I went back
I'd eat you up
I'd wreck the house
with my thousand-tipped horns
I'd slash
the flowerbeds to pieces
I'd rip up the trees
with my stag's teeth
I'd swallow the well
in one gulp—
if I went back
I'd set fire to the house
then I'd gallop off
to the burial plot
and with delicate nose
and all four hooves

I'd dig up my father—
I'd tear off the lid
of his coffin with my teeth—
I'd scatter his bones!
Mother, mother
Don't call me back,
I can't go back.
If I did go back,
I would kill you.

So the boy cried with a stag's voice,
and the mother answered him,
    come back, come back my son
I'm calling you, I, your own mother
    come back, my son, come back
I'll cook you sour-cabbage soup, you can slice onion-rings into it,
They'll crunch in your teeth like bits of stone in a giant's jaws,
I'll give you warm milk in a clean glass,
in my cellar the lair of fire-bellied frogs
in my cellar blinking like a giant green toad
I'll gently pour wine into heron-necked bottles,
with my stony fists I'll knead bread—for I know, I know
how to bake round little froth-bellied loaves, and Sunday twists—
    come back, come back my son
I plucked the crops of live, shrieking geese for your featherbed,
I cried I plucked the geese cried … the feather-wounds drooled white fat,
I sunned your straw mattress, I shook it out,
the clean-swept courtyard is listening for you, the table is laid.

    Aiii mother, mother
        I cannot go back,
    don't give me your twists of milk-loaf
        or sweet goat's milk in a flowered glass
    Don't make my bed springy and soft

or pluck out the throats of the geese—
throw the wine away, pour it over your father's grave
    weave the onions into a wreath,
fry your frothy doughnuts for the little ones now.
      For the warm milk would turn to vinegar in my mouth,
      a stone would squat in place of the milk loaf,
      the wine in my glass would turn to blood,
      each soft bed-feather become a flame,
      the small drinking mug a blade of blue sword-lily.
Aiii mother, aiii, aiii mother—
    I can't go back to my birthplace now.
Only the green forest can hold me,
    the house is too small for my huge, furry horns,
the courtyard has no space for my graveyard antlers,
    the shaking world-tree of my branching antlers
with stars as its leaves, the Milky Way as its moss.
    I can only eat sweet-smelling grass,
the tender young grass is my cud—
    I can no longer drink from a flowered glass,
only from a spring, only from a clean, fresh spring!

I don't understand, I don't understand your strange talk, son
you speak with a stag's voice, the soul of a stag moves in you, my poor one.
When the turtledove weeps, turtledove weeps, the little bird calls, little
                bird calls, my son
why am I, why am I in all creation the unhappy one?
Do you still remember, still remember your little mother, my son?
I don't understand, I don't understand your piteous crying, son.
Do you remember how happily you'd come running home, with your school-
                report,
you dissected frogs, nailed their speckled webby hands to the fence,
lost yourself in your airplane books, helped me in with the washing?
You were in love with Irena B … .V.J., and H.S. the painter, his beard like a
                wild orchid, was your friend.

Do you still remember, Saturday nights when your father came home sober,
how happy you were?

Aiii, mother, mother, don't remind me. My sweetheart and friends,
they swam from me cold like fish. The poppy-throated painter,
who knows where he went, mother—where my youth went?
Mother, mother don't mention my father. Sorrow flowers, blossoms from
his flesh of earth. Don't mention my father—
he'll get up from his grave, gather up his yellow bones
and come staggering out—his nails, his hair sprouting again.
Aiii, aiii! Old Wilhelm came, the coffin maker, runt with a doll's face.
He said, I'll grab your feet, we'll put you nicely into the box—
but I started retching with fear. I'd just come back from Pest,
you used to go there too, by train … a caretaker … the rails got twisted.
Aiii, I'd have cut myself to pieces, the candle puddling shadows on your
taut face—
Latzi, our new brother-in-law, the barber, shaved you. The candles drooled
like babies,
their innards melting out, dribbles, the bowels gleaming, the nerves
shining through.
The Choral Society stood around in their purple caps, lowing your
death like cattle,
and I touched your forehead. Your hair was alive,
I heard it grow, saw the bristles beginning on your chin—
by morning your chin was black, next day your throat was spiky like
stalks of viper's bugloss,
a slice of hairy melon, a yellow caterpillar with a blue-cabbage skin.
Aiii, I thought it would outgrow the room, the courtyard, the whole world
your beard and hair, the stars in it humming like vermin.
Aiii, aiii! In the dense green of rain, the red horses pulling your hearse
whinnied in fear—
one kicked out at your head, the other pissed helplessly, its purple
sex flopped out like a hanged man's tongue, the coachman swore,

rain washed the blare of the brass band, your mates were blowing and
        sobbing,
stood blowing by the thorny, thistled chapel wall,
blew out a basket of silvery breath from their puffed black lips,
blew the tune with cracked bloody lips and bloodshot eyes,
blew the card games, wines-and-sodas, the bloated and withered women,
blew the minted planets of coins, baksheesh, up into the void after you,
blew the thick dust of hopelessness away, sobbing. The tune
blared from the hard, glinting, O-mouthed horns into a void stinking
        of corpses—
petrified loves, decaying women, the moldering militias of grandfathers,
cottages, cradles, enamel and silver onion pocket-watches,
Easter bells multiplying redeemers like a bird's wing fanning,
trumpeting briefcases, train-wheels, brass-buttoned ratings stiff with
        salutes.
They blew with gum-pink teeth, the friends, with black puffy liver lips,
and you led them: That's it, lads! That's great! Aiii, don't stop playing—
your hands, crossed, a pair of golden spiders, long legs, jointed, hinged
        spokes of your heart.
Your shoes in the cupboard wait for the next-of-kin, your breadcrust-
        callous feet look childlike, helpless in their white socks,
and your mates blew on in the dashing rain, the trumpet-stops hic-
        cupped like steel adam's apples,
like claws of the reptile-bird, Carcharodon's teeth, the brass trumpets
        glittered.
Aiii, mother, mother, don't speak of my father.
    Leave him be, his eyes stare from the earth like buds.

The mother called to her own son,
    cried, from far away
come back my son, come back
    come away from that stone world
stag of the stone forest, smogs, electric grids and neon glitter.
    The iron bridges and tramlines, they thirst for your blood,

a hundred times a day they jab you, but you never hit back—
I am calling you, I, your own mother
    come back my son, come back.

There he stood on the crest of all time,
there he stood on creation's highest mountain,
there he stood at the gate of secrets—
the points of his antlers played with the stars
and with a stag's voice he cried,
cried back to his mother who'd borne him—
    mother, mother, I can't go back
the hundred wounds in me weep pure gold,
I die every day, a hundred bullets in me
every day I get up again a hundred times stronger
I die every day three billion deaths
and three billion times a day I am born,
each prong of my antlers a twin-legged pylon
each branch of my antlers a high-tension wire,
my eyes are ports of cargo-ships, my veins are greased cables,
my teeth are iron bridges, my heart is a thrashing ocean of monsters,
each vertebra is a thriving city, my spleen is a chuffing stone-barge,
each cell is a vast factory, every atom a solar system,
my testicles are the sun and moon, the Milky Way is my spine-marrow,
each point in space is one grain of my body,
each galaxy an inkling of my brain.

Son, my lost son, I still want you back—
    your mother's eyes, like a dragonfly's, won't rest until you come.

To die I'll come back, only to die.
To die I'll come back,
mother—only to die will I come.
Then you can lay me out in my childhood home,
with your age-veined hands you can wash my body,

close my eyelids, swollen glands, with kisses.
    And when the flesh falls off me,
and the stench it was sweetens to flowers,
    I'll be a fetus drinking your blood,
I'll be your little boy again—
and this hurts only you, mother,
    aiii, hurts only you, mother.

Hunger and Hate

If there were a god I'd deny him.
I'd hammer the dead flesh of his face.
I'd snap at his hand like a dog as he stooped
to pat me. With tears and a gun I'd waylay him.

I'd take a rainbow-quick sliver
of glass, and gouge his balls out.
I'd slash at his groin till the pain
was red-hot and his blood gushed rust like oil.

I'd gnaw at his shinbone
with its spidery hairs, a mad dog
foaming away the obedient centuries—

then I'd yank his heart out, like the shark
biting through all the ages of fish on the hook—
a greasy stomach, a mottled blue fin.

Four Seasons

Autumn is gone. The leaves have turned to mold.
I tramped over the mush of plants on my way to you.
My orphaned eyes skulked in holes the dead had abandoned
like hermit crabs in the dead shells they crawl to.
The whale-mouthed iron railings dribbled violet shadows of the dead,
spongy babies, stale chrysanthemums, hung from their lips, moaning and crying.
They brought me a blue turtledove, a gold chain and a bell on its tiny leg.
I drowned in your atom-splitting smile, your moongaze turned my hair grey.

And winter's over. Not like winters we knew.
A sky of bone crackles in the jaws of the church bells.
Teeth chattering like machine guns I went out begging crumbs for you.
The still forest glittered like broken glass.
Shadows blue as hyacinth blurred from the frosted railings,
and grieving, hooded in quiet, the animals, tiptoeing, circled your window.
By the bed I listened to your breezy chatter, like a jasmine rustling,
and red deer, hare, pheasant, thrush, heard the white flame of your song in the churned
snow.

And now it is spring. A soft mold-flush
oozes and sticks to the walls in a thin green glaze.
Dead flower heads drift and soak in the jelly mush,
and death circles in from the void, misting the eyes.
The blotchy railings vomit bile-green shadows
where man-eating fish and stars with shark's teeth swirl home to the feast,
brought by sick lusts and stale prayers, mad gibberings and curses.
And I, an elder tree on your dead-alive grave, throw myself on the stelae of your breasts.

Summer will come, minting us gold with light.
On the moon the magic unicorn rears with his blue grin.
And the wailing world remembers its griefs, the nerves tensing around it.

In its ultraviolet scum, the insect breeds to distraction;
acid shadows drip from the peeling railings,
and butterflies burn to ash on your heart, as the lizard's fist squeezes it.
In this garden of ferns I hear your girl-flower weeping.
In this cave of blood-red stones I moan to you, a black leopard buried alive in your heart.

The Flower of Silence

The flower of silence fades to grief's huge funeral leaves
Don't cry don't scream don't tear me apart with your eyes
Don't tie me to the grieving cross with live ropes weeping blood
I'm drying up my flesh my glands death is a shimmer of flies

My nerve-tentacles weave through the dripping stars
Squeezing and sucking the blood of starfish I'm drunk
I'm a mad green eye whirled on the poles of its grief
Help me my carnivore mask has eaten away my face

Go back to the forest I heard the song of the stag
Silence is every leaf the trees grow noiselessly
Peace is a wandering doe the birds are scarlet flowers
My heart seed of your heart the flower of silence opens.

A Church in Bulgaria

Inside a church in Batak in 1876,
4,000 Bulgarians were massacred by the Turks.

Wreathed into the earth, a stone coffin, this church,
an unbreakable stone bubble:
it wants to flutter away, soar in the air

but is torn by its dead weight down into the soil—
earth gnaws at its solid mass
through the spidery roots which suckle it too.
Like a horse's skull stripped of its glory of flesh,
the past! a grinning skull
which the humus hasn't buried quite—
humus, the earth, the oval cropland
which whirls with us, rolls in the burning dust of space.
And what's kept there, hoarded
deep, as in men's hearts? What's buried there,
dragged down into itself incalculable
millions of years: silence which won't complain?
Bone, vertebra, skull, self-sweat,
metal, coal and fern;
earth's earliest beasts crystallized in unknown layers,
flowers of the far past, fish cut in stone,
old anthems, shards of forgotten epics
and again: bone, vertebra, skull,
whole millennia of flaking eyes,
prehistoric fish-rot, gases, oils,
statues the marble limbs of dead cities
lost in the stale and fresh strata, they jab at the earth from beneath;
and lava, the liquid fire earth spews at will.
This seeps from the earth, earth dries it, like sweat on a thinking head,
or a mammoth brain its own thoughts,
time without end.

Earth I stand on, here, bloodsoaked stones
I won't pry deeper, or ask more of your past.
The lesson is here, in the blood-ruined beams
of this stone skull blown by man's brain, walls clenched under its weight
like old men's shoulders already bending
under, to earth. There they'll fall. Where the stones grew
was man's source too: he was cast up from it

like the fish from water. Above him the dust tides over
unruffled, still: just rolls with a smothering rumble.

For they're here too: bones, vertebrae, skulls, a yellow
heap in the marble coffin's belly of mirrors[1]—
bones, vertebrae, skulls. Look, like a lime-bubble
or water-bead: white bones with a baby's head,
or an old man's, like a black sod,
a tiny shinbone, knotty and yellow and
hollow like a straw; a carious, fat
starshape vertebra, twisted fingerbones,
a skull drilled with bullet holes
like a maggoty fruit, a virgin's delicate
knotted kneecap, like a walking stick—all one spiky heap
like a hayrick pitched over stakes out on a lake.
For the coffin's reflecting belly of mirrors
flashes one lesson a thousand ways—
bone, vertebra, skull.

What happened here? What does this crying emblem
mean, here in the heart of the church this once-
soul and marrow-gifted crown?
It mourns the madness of power, greed, pride—and the dignity
of defiance, passion of man and woman,
for you, you earth, the fiery unquenchable core in us
        Liberty!

The defiance whose eyes would drill through rock
rather than smile for dictators.
Man's stubbornness is such
he'd sooner gnash his tongue to a bloody
spittle than thank his oppressors.

---

[1] The custom of placing the bones of saints in mirror-lined coffins occurs in the Greek Orthodox Church.
D. W.

And the courage: woman who'd show her full white breasts
like the Carpathian heights under snow,
as a mocking gift to the knives christian or
infidel—but cries "Be damned to you, murderer!"
And the honor, this hairy male-breast
more muscular than the chest of a horse, he
bares to their guns, steel weaker than his gaze.

Here the blood rose high as their heads, trembling—
dome and window moist with its ruby steam,
in this church, the eye of a dragonfly husk.
Here it stood, a black jelly of fear,
the slaughtered patriots' blood—
men, women and children who stood
silently frowning, victims watching
this blood-rampage of power.
For the human heart endures much
but can't live in its iron bands forever—
suddenly it flares up like a dying star,
anger gushing energy in a shower of fire.
Which is what these did: the downtrodden
raised their arms and eyes against the oppressor.

O he knew already the game was over,
the trick lost, the dice gone dead in his hand!
So before he'd crouch terrified over the horse's mane
and escape on the stallion flying with swollen nostrils and veins
sweating crimson froth, he held,
here, a last feast, a human pig-killing.
For still he craved flesh, lusted to be drunk
on the steaming crimson broth, that magic stallion.
Drop by drop he filled the stone communion cup with blood.
This blood-guzzling, this stony eucharist, is history now.

The seared villages, fired huts,
virgins spitted on swords, women
with marble skins ripped by diamond spear-holes,
broken lilies, gouged eyes
weeping like squashed plums—
these visions, like the mica-flakes of the Milky Way
remain, to haunt the child of a later century.
As here, now: the bones, vertebrae, skulls, heaped up
holy reminder and lesson,
in this church shocked to stone.
Bones, vertebrae, skulls … enough.
Can my senses still live with this sight,
this heaped imagery of horror?
Is there one cell left in my body
which hasn't suffered the death these bones did?

Is there a cell in my brain
that isn't part of this grandeur now?
Have you an ounce of shame left,
poet? Shame for yourself
as you stand here, in a white shirt, a summer suit,
on the stones of this church in August '52?

A Message Too Late

I read your poems again, my friend.
I read them slowly, line by line,
thumbing the pages, thinking of you, my friend.
And why deny it? I wept at the thought of your name.
I wasn't sorting them, sheep from goats
like a mustering of autumn conscripts—
I just gave up and stared at the massed rows

of your poems, your whole identity, friend.
Here your dry X-ray sight opens
the cave-dwellers' lair, and the flowers of doubt,
and the wings of the pterodactyl, flesh-eater, bird-father,
to get at the secrets of the human heart.
Like the surgeon in Rembrandt's picture
you showed us dissection, you raped a dead world's nerves.
How you must have sweated days,
bringing those nightmare facts to life!
Hunched over the corpse's rainbow guts
by the light of the smelly oil lamp in your cellar,
your dry obsession made your fingers itch—
but in the end, what can a corpse tell you?
Well it's here, we see it. You forced us to see.
Now what will cleanse the infection from our eyes?
You never forgave us our wrongheadedness—
but is there no hope? Not one refreshing word?
Just one word as clear as the rain
that gives birth to a homeland or curses a world?

Black Peacock

Points, angles, hollows, lines, all
meet in this head: rough-chiseled, its veins still showing.
The eye is ringed with a deep
moat of sadness, a trench hammered out of tin.

Remember, Pishta, the winter nights would cry—
"Even Jesus shouldered his own green tree!
Someone's kissing Pishta's girl, and it isn't he!"

Lurching like an old gravestone,

he rubs against the nudging shoulders of women.
His tears are knives with mother-of-pearl handles.
His words kindle timeless shivers under their skin.

Pishta, old friend, remember when we sat
on the Danube embankment, on top of that marble post,
and love wailed and cried like something lost.

He has no father or mother.
Perhaps God dreamed him up
to ease his own conscience. But when he turns
to dust the Phoenix is born, the snowdrop opens.

Remember, Pishta, remember
the sky was a wireless bringing us news, it was winter,
we wept: can one still kiss and play the lover?

On his heart a black peacock struts and cries.
Talk to him … he lurches away, won't answer.
Won't talk, but listens for the peacock step.
Does nothing but cry, in the spell of the peacock's cry.

Remember, Pishta, old friend of mine,
those days when love was like a bottle of wine,
a moonlit track cutting through snow and pine.

Girls, don't tear him to pieces
like convicts squabbling over a loaf of bread.
Griefs, don't rant and scrabble around him
like furies over the heart of a dying man.

Pishta, remember the other day
I swore I would let myself waste away
if I didn't find my life's share of joy?

Now those who can love, and kill for love,
have time enough to hate him,
if from this bundle of points, angles, hollows
and lines, only silence, numbness, is left of him.

The Rainbow-Colored Whale

Now your grave is sinking,
like your back
when the scalpel
cut away your ribs.

They say, the wreath
we laid at your head has withered,
the plank's gone rotten
that propped your dead heart.

Your grave is sinking deeper,
a black mouth lying in wait.
Every day I bring fresh earth
in a big willow basket.

But the earth I bring in the evening
is gone by morning;
the earth I bring in the morning
by nightfall has sunk without trace.

As if you were eating
and eating your way through the earth,
forever upwards,
with those toothless gums.

The salt-spray eating the coral
becomes the coral—
the worm devoured you,
now you devour the worm.

You eat through it all
like a huge grub,
insatiable mouth without stomach,
munching into daylight.

Tons of stones and clay—
nothing can stop those jaws!
What can you want in our world
with your dead will?

Skull, Nothing,
what is it you want?
Learn the final lesson.
You are alone now.

Rainbow-colored whale,
swimming the waters under the earth,
obey the laws of the earth,
the vows of death and burial.

Earth swallowed you whole,
and you swallowed the whole world.
No hope, no body left—
it's time you understood.

Rainbow-colored whale, thrashing and
churning the clogged waters under the earth,
you are a predator now,
not worthy of what you were.

When you were alive your skin
was a breathing marsh of colors,
your sweat gushed in little
squirts, like hypodermics.

But you haven't noticed
how naked you've grown,
how the black earth
has melted you.

Those cold eyes that knew
the stone-green world of boulder and pine
have burst by now,
soft, like seaweed pods.

You didn't even know
they'd betrayed you—
sold every ounce of you
for Judas-gold!

The traces left in the air
by your wandering desires—
gone forever,
under the hoarfrost.

And whatever sediment remained
of your heart
has been turned to stone,
melted away with the waters.

Little by little
time has eaten
the tartar from your teeth,
the grief from your eyes.

And it's time you learnt
not to see hope in such signs.
When a man dies,
he loses his will to live.

My grief for you was like thorns,
but the thorns have withered.
The green tree of your absence
is slowly beginning to flower.

The tusks of the black boar,
the tusks of the black boar that
slashed you open—
the sting has gone out of the wound.

But why were you never
as hungry as this—
so hungry I feel you
unwinding out of the grave?

No man has the right
to live it all over again!
I haven't the strength
to bury you twice!

Look, your sea's dried up—
don't thrash about
in the earth's black surf
as if it were water.

You'd swallow the sun
like a goldfish?
Strain the sumac tree
through your teeth, like parsley?

Bone-flower,
burrowing towards the light,
don't ever blossom. Don't gnaw
into our moonlight with your rat's teeth.

Larva,
don't eat your way into my heart.
I live with your absence.
You don't exist.

Life here is peaceful
without you.
Flower then, flower into
the death-wish of the lily.

Thursday, Day of Superstition

On the third day it is hardest, on the third.

Distracted, nowhere to go,
I roam this island of stone and neon, the Octagon.
It is Thursday evening,
no time for cursing,
no time for crying.

Red, blue, yellow, green, the rain is falling.
The streets are rainbows
riddled with pattering bubbles.
The bubble-creatures roll their eyes
like chameleons, round and round
as a pebble rolls in a clay jar.
Their watery skins

ripple from color to color—
the lizards of rain crawl all over each other.
This island is Galapagos,
this lonely flowering of stones.

I am alone.

The island spins like a huge merry-go-round.
Taxis, buses, trams—step up for the joyride!
The shop-fronts whirl round and round like drunken stars.
The sword-lilies are whores in this amusement park.

Red, blue, yellow, green, the rain is falling.
The news-vendors are shouting.
The flower-sellers say nothing.

To the rooftops, silent, glowing,
animal-flowers are climbing the scaffolding—
night's instant creatures,
the neon monsters.

My heart sees its fate crucified on the sky—
a twinkling map of neon,
a huge technicolor brain,
Hungary.

Its villages, its towns,
brain cells, needles of light,
electric rivers of blue veins,
convolutions of land and brain.

I'M LOSING MY MIND!

On the third day it is hardest, on the third.

No time for cursing.
No time for crying.

But the rain is flowering a roof,
patches of wall, a hint of sky where
a tiny spider of light hangs in its web of light.
And through the dripping light-cells crawls
the mimosa leaf of advertisements,
opening, twirling, closing
like a sea-anemone's head…
slowly it sways,
feeling its way.

HELP ME SOMEONE!

But through the dripping rain-
ferns, monsters are crawling…
nylon, plastic and rubber
skins, hiss
and crackle and shine in the light as they move.

Women in lizard skins.
Men in snake skins.

They hunger.
And they thirst.

A bestiary
of red, blue, green and yellow faces.

Who knows me standing here in the cold?
Who will accept my gift of flowers?
Who are my friends? Where have they gone?
My voice is a shout in a dream.

I search the rain,
looking for you.
A blue voice calling you, calling you.

From the red, yellow and green
scribbles of light,
night sketches a shape in the rain—
a giant beer mug.
It has just a minute to live.

The amber beer sparkles like fire.
Neon lather slops over the rim
vomiting, dribbling yellow stains
of frothing electricity into the rain.

Where am I going?
What song am I singing?

"Save me, O Lord, from all evil"

On the third day it is hardest, on the third.

What am I doing here?
Where else is there?

I flounder around in the swill of neon beer.
But I feel like a child wanting to scream,
to be given something … and how the world would laugh!
O Hungary I'd climb the neon veins of your body and skull,
I'd sprawl on your neon brain
so the world could see in radiance through my ribs
my beating heart's blister,
your own heart.

No, it is not permitted.

On the third day it is hardest, on the third.

No time for cursing,
no time for weeping.
In this wilderness of rainbow and rain
I hear my grandmother's voice again—
"Save me, Lord, from the unicorn, the four-breasted bird
Save me, Lord, from the mangy ram and the whinnying flower
Save me, Lord, from the barking toad and the hooved angel
Save me O Lord, save me from all evil"

But who's there? Who am I talking to?
Who can save himself with a song?
I denied God. I laughed him away.
I flicked his balls with thorns and ran like a street-boy.
I've blown my tiny flame
to a tree of fire, ten miles high—
and the scorched insects fall like ash from the sky.
Red, blue, green,
I wear as my laurels this neon wreath,
I drown in the purple beard of a neon man
whose tentacles lick through my skull to devour the brain.

Only you can save me, you.
On the third day it is hardest, on the third.

What do I want?
What did I ever want?
I dug myself into your heart
like a soldier, numbed by the shells,
deeper and deeper into the mud of your heart
under the grinning jack o' lantern
skulls, and the shrapnel leafing like trees
all around me…flies dabbing the blood

from the rags and swaying vines of flesh and veins
and rainbow lids and eyes twitching like flowers.

I lie curled
like a question, an embryo,
in the drumming jungle of your blood.
Your ribs sway softly like a crib,
but your heavy heartbeat shakes me,
the pulse and clutch of your entrails shakes me.
I hear the cauldron of your liver,
the sweat of your kidneys dripping phosphor;
my eye is the risen moon in your night,
its tentacles probing
for dawn in the dark of your body.
You are the depths of space and ocean to me.

I'm alone.

You are with me.

Red, blue, yellow, green …
still the rain is falling.
The sea is swirling full of phosphorous eyes.
The sea's brain, Hungary,
is a neon medusa drifting above me,
and our world, an anemone lost in the chaos of space
swims round and round in a gulf of the Milky Way.

Larva,
I know you'll shed your skin.
Your gift is flight. You will begin
stretching your frail new amber wings,
unfurling them from their glues of birth,
and their fibers will dry in the warm wind

as the wings flutter, fanning free of the blue slime—
and the womb of time will close behind
you. I know, because our fates are the same.

I'm alone.
I bow my rainsoaked head.

On the third day it is hardest, on the third.
It is Thursday evening,
no time for cursing,
no time for weeping.

Hell-bent on life, like a sponge, I head for home
in the red, green and blue rain: in the age of socialism.

A Note on Fernando Pessoa, San Juan de la Cruz, and Alberto de Lacerda

Nearly all the translations here were done with the help and collaboration of scholars and native speakers. The Pessoa poems are the work of Alberto de Lacerda and myself equally, and appeared originally under both our names. A native of Portugal, Fernando Pessoa (1888–1935) claimed that Álvaro de Campos, Alberto Caeiro, and Ricardo Reis were not pseudonyms but deep, uncontrollable expressions of his personalities, or *heteronimós* as he called them. The names of the presiding *heteronimós* have been noted at the bottom of each of the Pessoa poems in this volume.

The life and artistic accomplishment of Spanish poet and mystic San Juan de la Cruz (1542–1591) is too vast to do justice to in this briefest of introductions. The Baroque Renaissance Spanish of San Juan de la Cruz is impossible to capture in anything like readable, modern English. I feel that my translation of "The Dark Night" is a quieter, more lyrical version than the typical representations of this great poem.

Born in Mozambique, Alberto de Lacerda (1928–2007) was one of Portugal's most distinguished and admired poets. During his lifetime, de Lacerda worked as an announcer for the BBC, freelance journalist, teacher (both at the University of Texas at Austin and Boston University), critic, and translator. My versions of Alberto de Lacerda's poems were done with his help and guidance, though the responsibility for the final versions is mine alone.

D. W.

Fernando Pessoa
After the Fair

They wander down the road
Singing for no reason,
A final gift of hope
For the ultimate illusion.
They don't mean anything.
They are only fools and mimes.

They go, together and
Singly through the moonlight,
Lost in some dream
They will never know,
Singing the words of these poems
That come to mind.

Pages from some dead myth,
So lyrical, so lonely!
No cry breaks their voices,
The voices are scarcely their own.
And the infinite has never
Heard of them, or of us.

Fernando Pessoa

Every day I discover

Every day I discover
The incredible reality of things.
Each thing is what it is,

Intact; and it's hard to explain to someone how much
This delights and fills me.
To exist is enough to be whole.

I have written so many poems.
Of course I shall write many more.
Every poem of mine says this,
And none of my poems is the same,
Since everything that exists is another way of saying it.

Sometimes I'll look at a stone.
I am not concerned whether a stone can feel.
The stone is not my sister —
I like it because it is a stone,
Because it feels nothing
And is no relation of mine.

Other times I hear the wind passing.
I think it is worth being born, to hear the passing wind.

I don't know what the world will make of this.
But I feel it is true, because thinking this way
Is my nature; and no one
Can hear me thinking.
My thoughts live only in words.

Once I was called a
"materialist poet"—surprised
That my soul had a name.
I am no poet, I just have eyes.
If my words matter, the matter is there
In my poems, not in me. My will
Is no part of my poems. They exist.

Alberto Caeiro

Henry the Navigator

On his throne among the shining spheres,
In his cloak of night and solitude,
At his feet the new ocean, and the past ages—
He is the one emperor
Who truly holds the world's globe in his hand.

Fernando Pessoa

Ode

To be great you must be whole. Don't
Exaggerate or leave things out.
Be whole in everything, put your whole
Self into the smallest thing you do.
So the full moon, from her height,
Shines over every lake.

Ricardo Reis

On a Book Abandoned on a Journey

I came from near Beja.
I am going straight into Lisbon
bringing nothing with me: and I shall find nothing.
I am weary with what I shall not find,
and the longing I feel is neither for present nor future.
I record, here, this image of myself:
I existed, like grass, and I was not uprooted.

Álvaro de Campos

San Juan de la Cruz
The Dark Night

On a dark night
love's anguish burning in me
O blessed risk
I went out, no one saw me
the house now quiet and still

Safely in the dark
by the secret ladder, disguised
O blessed chance
hidden in the dark
my house now quiet and still

In the night blest with secrecy
for no one saw me
and my self saw nothing
led by no other light
but what burned in my heart to guide me

which led me on
more surely than the light of noon
to where someone waited
whom I knew intimately
in a place where no one came

O night that led me on
night more obliging than any dawn
O night bringing together
the lover and the loved one
the beloved transformed in the Lover

On my flowering breast
kept only and wholly for him
he lay sleeping
while I caressed him
fanned by breezes form the cedar trees

A breeze off the parapets,
then as I spread out his hair
with a hand light as air
he touched and hurt my neck,
and all my senses hung there

I stayed, I forgot myself
I laid my face against my Lover.
Everything stopped, my self
my cares behind me
among the lilies forgotten.

Alberto de Lacerda
Four

Man and geometry
the light
and the sword

man
and geometry
the light and the sword

man

    geometry

        light

          sword

man and light
geometry
and the sword

light
and man
geometry   and the sword

(man) light
(man) sword

the gods

Yucatán—Mexico
28 Dec. '69

Bones of man

Bones of man
Bones of woman

The pyramid stairs prolong
its subterranean flight

down
to the dark-

most
galleries
of the blood

> *Mérida*—Yucatán
> 29 Dec. '69

In Hadrian's Palace

This is a temple of absolute love
whole, like marble or water
that do not hesitate, make no mistakes

This is the palace of a love born
ancient, limitless, without question or
answer. Oneself's gift, everything,
soul: meeting herself at the knife-
edge, where the horizon overflows

This is the palace of Hadrian
the temple of Antinous

the palace of love, tender, love, child,
adult, and so deepened, death
suddenly gave it back
to be immortal

Villa Adriana—Italy
10 Aug. '69

Poem for Octavio Paz

Where the conjunction is
                              disjointed
mutilated snake
of time

eating its own tail

Mérida—Yucatán
31 Dec. '69

Here

Here

time
exists

stone
phallus, visible

from all four corners of

creation

Mérida—Yucatán
31 Dec. '69

Palace of Piero Della Francesca

I

This place is sacred. Grace, here
unfolding image, stone
apparitions on skin of water. Fish
multiplied nameless dance
Queen of Sheba
                    Throne
                              A naked
boy, his back turned

blue light, and the silence white
news of another sea and depth
where dance, motionless, innocent
incarnate presence

II

This place, is sacred. Grace here
unfolding, image, fish
apparitions on skin of stone. Fish
multiplied nameless dance
stone, fish, stone, faceted,

thrones
        battles
              columns
                    dividing
not tragic, the light, indivisible, light

Arezzo—Italy
16 Aug. '69

Your beauty hurts

Your beauty hurts
               silence beyond
that open door

Austin—Texas
2 Oct. '69

Ceremony

Dance is the gesture
In which man touches
The palm of the hand of the god

New Mexico
22 Mar. '70

Sun within

Sun within
sun without

internal sun bestowing
external sun bestowing demanding

snake
uncoiling towards the sun

the root colors
resolved in the pillar of sun

sun
in majesty

> Mexico City
> 21 Dec. '69

About the Editor

Michael McGriff was born and raised in Coos Bay, Oregon. He is the author of the poetry collection *Dismantling the Hills* and co-translator (with Mikaela Grassl) of Tomas Tranströmer's *The Sorrow Gondola*. He has received many awards for his work, including a National Endowment for the Arts Fellowship, a Stegner Fellowship, a Ruth Lilly Fellowship, and a James A. Michener Fellowship. His poetry and translations have appeared in *American Poetry Review*, *The Believer*, *Slate*, *Agni*, and *Field*, among other publications. He is currently a Jones Lecturer at Stanford University.

Index of Titles

Index of First Lines